Our America....
The Pilgrim Adventure

For some free activity ideas to accompany this
book, visit the author's website at
http://funtasticunitstudies.com/

ALSO BY SUSAN KILBRIDE

Science Unit Studies for Homeschoolers and Teachers

Our America....

The Pilgrim Adventure

Susan Kilbride

Funtastic Unit Studies
USA

http://funtasticunitstudies.com/

Our America....
The Pilgrim Adventure
Copyright © 2012 by Susan Kilbride

The front cover is adapted from:
The Mayflower Approaching Land, Marshall Johnson, published by John A. Lowell, Boston 1905

Distributors and retailers can purchase this book directly from the publisher at:
www.createspace.com/info/createspacedirect

ISBN-13: 978-1470037987

ISBN-10: 147003798X

Acknowledgements

First and foremost, I would like to thank my husband and son for being so patient with me while I am using the computer. This book would never have been written without their love and support. I would also like to thank my son for his great help in proof-reading my manuscripts. I first gave him the job as a schooling lesson, but soon found that he was very good at catching my errors!

I would also like to thank everyone who gave me so much encouragement with my first book, *Science Unit Studies for Homeschoolers and Teachers.* To all of the people who took the time to review it or post information about it, I thank you so much. Your praise and kind words encouraged me to try my hand at writing another book for homeschoolers and teachers.

And special thanks to my parents and sister who have always been my biggest cheerleaders, and to Joe Legueri my inspirational high school English teacher.

Thank you all, I couldn't have done it without you!

Susan Kilbride

1

Uncle Peter Disappears

Twelve-year-old Ginny sat at the kitchen table doing her schoolwork while her twin brother Finn stared at the forest outside of their aunt and uncle's cabin home. Suddenly, Finn jumped up and shouted in surprise.

"What's wrong?" Ginny exclaimed.

"Uncle Peter--he was standing in front of that tree, and then he just disappeared!"

"You must have fallen asleep or something; he couldn't have disappeared."

"But he did, I saw it," Finn insisted.

"Well he's not there now, and you'd better hurry up and get your work done so we can go to the fair this afternoon," Ginny said.

Finn sighed and turned back to his work. Both Finn and Ginny were homeschooled, and their Aunt Martha had told them that they couldn't go to the fair until their work for the day was done. Finn was especially looking forward to the fair as his best friend Jack was going to be there, and Jack had some parts that Finn needed to complete the robot he was building.

Just then the twins heard footsteps coming down the stairs, and their Uncle Peter walked into the room. Finn looked up in surprise, "How did you get into the house so fast?" he demanded.

"What do you mean?" replied Uncle Peter.

"I just saw you outside by that tree a minute ago, and then suddenly you came down the stairs."

Uncle Peter just smiled and opened the refrigerator door. "If you kids want to go to the fair, you'd better get ready!" he said.

Finn and Ginny cleaned up their books and ran upstairs. "I know what I saw" Finn grumbled. Ginny looked at him. A boy-version of her own face looked back at her; dark brown hair and brown eyes that had a sad cast to them. "I wonder if my eyes look that sad" she thought. "Ever since Mom and Dad disappeared, Finn's eyes have had that sad look, and I suppose mine do too."

It seemed like just yesterday when Finn and Ginny's parents had told them that they were all going to visit Uncle Peter and Aunt Martha for Christmas. They had been so excited to go spend a Christmas in the woods! Uncle Peter and Aunt Martha's house was built like a large cabin and was nestled in the middle of a forest in Northern Wisconsin. And it *had* been lots of fun, right up until the day their parents disappeared. Ginny and Finn woke up one morning, and their parents weren't there. At first everyone thought that they had just gone for a walk, but as time went on, it became obvious that something bad had happened to them. And now, over a year later, it appeared that they were never coming back. Uncle Peter and Aunt Martha were Finn and Ginny's only living relatives, so they had given the children a home, but that didn't fill the void of their missing parents. Every morning when Ginny woke up and remembered that her parents were missing, her heart hurt.

Later that evening, Finn and Ginny were sitting in Ginny's room reading. Finn looked up. "Ginny, I did see Uncle Peter disappear; I wasn't asleep, and I wasn't imagining things. And it's not the first time that I've seen him do that."

"What do you mean?" asked Ginny.

"Last week I was coming down the stairs and he was standing by the fireplace, then suddenly he sort of dissolved away."

Ginny looked worriedly at Finn. "I think that maybe you're stressed out about Mom and Dad and it's affecting your brain or something."

Finn looked at her angrily, "This has nothing to do with Mom and Dad! I know what I saw!" Suddenly, he stopped and looked thoughtfully at her. "Then again, perhaps you are right; what if it does have something to do with Mom and Dad? What if they disappeared like Uncle Peter, but they never came back?!"

Ginny stared at him in shock. This actually made more sense to her than the thought that her parents had just upped and left them. Both her parents had seemed so happy; she knew that they loved her and Finn very much and that they never would have left them of their own accord. "Let's talk to Uncle Peter," she said.

The children slowly walked down the stairs and went into the cozy living room where Uncle Peter and Aunt Martha sat by the fireplace. Aunt Martha had graying hair, with a kind face and a beautiful smile. Uncle Peter was tall with dark brown hair like the twins, and brown eyes that twinkled when he laughed. They both looked up at the children as they came down the stairs.

Aunt Martha looked at them in concern. "Is anything wrong dears?" she asked.

The twins stood in front of Uncle Peter, and Finn said, "We think that it's time you told us what is going on."

Uncle Peter stared at them. "What are you talking about?"

"I've watched you disappear and then re-appear again later, and I think it has something to do with what happened to our parents. I'm tired of not knowing what's happened to them and I think that you owe us an explanation!" Finn said loudly.

Uncle Peter kept looking at them. "Well, if you are old enough to figure that out, perhaps you are old enough to learn the truth," he said.

Aunt Martha started to rise from her chair, "Now Peter..."

"No Martha, we need to tell them. Finn's right, they deserve to know." He turned to the children, "Sit down kids, it's a long story."

Finn and Ginny sat and stared at their Uncle as he started to pace around the room. "You see kids, a number of years ago I became concerned with how the history of our country seemed to be getting forgotten. I felt that something had to be done to remind people of who we are and how we came to be here, and of what a great country this really is. I decided that the first step would be for me to really learn our history myself. As you know, I like inventing things and so I decided to try and invent a time machine."

"What the..." Finn exclaimed. "You've got to be kidding right?!"

"No, I'm not Finn," said Uncle Peter. "It took me a long time, but after many years I finally had my time machine. I was going to show it to your parents when they were here, but I was waiting until the right moment. Unfortunately, they found it before I had a chance to show it to them, and they must have accidently turned it on and gone back in time."

Ginny jumped up and started yelling at her uncle. "Stop this, stop this right now! If you don't want to tell us where they are, don't, but don't lie to us; don't make up stories!"

Aunt Martha got up, grabbed Ginny and looked into her eyes. "Ginny, he's not lying, it's true."

Ginny's mouth dropped open and she slowly sank back into her chair. She knew that Aunt Martha *never* lied. "It can't be true, it can't be."

"Unfortunately it is," said Uncle Peter.

"Well, let's go get them back," exclaimed Finn, "Let's get them right now. What are we waiting for?"

"It's not that easy," Uncle Peter explained. "You see, first, I don't know what time period they went to. And second, I don't know where they went to. They could be anytime and anywhere in our country. I've been trying every day since they left to find them, but I just haven't had any luck."

"How do you know that they even used the time machine?" asked Ginny.

Uncle Peter looked sadly at her. "When we woke up that morning, the time machine was lying on the floor in this room. I had put it in the drawer by the end table to show your parents, but we had gotten distracted that night and I didn't get a chance. They must have thought it was a TV remote and tried to use it that morning. I have no idea where they are."

2

The Adventure Begins

That night Ginny was lying in bed, staring up at the luminous stars she and Aunt Martha had painted on her ceiling, when she heard a soft knock on her bedroom door.

"Ginny, it's me, can I come in?" she heard her brother whisper. She sat up as he crept through the door. "Ginny, I'm not going to just sit here and wait for Uncle Peter to find Mom and Dad; he's been trying for a year now and hasn't found them. I want to go look for them myself."

"Not without me you aren't!" Ginny exclaimed. "They're my parents too you know!"

Finn grinned at her, "I thought you might feel that way; in fact I was counting on it. It's much more fun going on an adventure with company!

Our first step is to find the time machine, and tomorrow is the perfect day for it. Uncle Peter has to go to work and Aunt Martha will be taking photos at the Sorenson's wedding."

"That's right!" exclaimed Ginny, "I'd forgotten that. But we're supposed to go to Jack's house for the day."

"Jack's mom called; he's got a fever, so we'll be staying here by ourselves tomorrow."

"That's perfect!" said Ginny. "We can search the house for the time machine. Uncle Peter said it looked like a TV remote, so it shouldn't be too hard to spot." The twins grinned at each other and started making plans. Later, as Ginny fell asleep, she felt for the first time in a while that maybe she would finally see her parents again.

* * * *

The next morning Aunt Martha turned to them and asked for what felt like the hundredth time, "Are you sure you two will be o.k. here on your own all day?"

"Don't worry about us Aunt Martha, we'll be fine," said Finn.

"Well, don't forget to feed the chickens, and make sure that you both clean your rooms."

"Yes Aunt Martha," the twins chorused as they waved goodbye.

Once they were alone Finn turned to Ginny, "Let's start; you search the upstairs, and I'll search the downstairs. We'll collect everything we find that looks like a remote, but don't try and use it until we are both together."

"Good plan, let's go!"

Two hours later the twins were sitting in the living room nervously looking at the pile of remotes in front of them.

"Do you think it might be here?" asked Ginny.

"I don't know, but if it is, I bet it's this one."

"What's so special about that one?"

"I found it in a sock in Uncle Peter's dresser. Why would he hide a regular remote in a sock?"

They both stared at the remote. It looked almost like a normal TV remote, except that it had a tiny screen at the top and two buttons on it that said "Go" and "Home."

"Uncle Peter said that Mom and Dad got lost because they dropped the remote; so they couldn't use it to get back. We'll have to make sure that whatever happens, we don't drop it," Ginny said.

"I think we should pack some supplies before we go anywhere. Let's go get our backpacks and load them up with food and maybe some other things."

"Good idea!"

As Ginny filled her backpack with food, she realized that they were both very scared about the adventure that they were about to go on. But then she thought of her parents, lost in the past somewhere, and she forced her mind to concentrate on getting ready instead of worrying about what could happen.

Back at the remote, Peter handed her a fanny pack. "We'll keep the remote in this when we get there. We don't want to lose it." Ginny silently took the fanny pack and put it on.

The twins looked at each other. Then they put on their backpacks. Ginny grabbed on to Finn's arm.

"Are you ready?" Finn asked, with his finger poised over the "Go" button. Ginny nodded and Finn pressed the button. Suddenly the lights seemed to go out, the world started spinning, and the twin's stomachs felt like they were dropping off of a cliff. It was all Ginny could do to hang on to Finn's arm. There was no time to think or wonder if they had done the right thing; there was only fear, chaos, and nausea.

3

On Board Ship

The twins suddenly landed with such a hard thump that the wind was knocked out of them and they couldn't breathe. As they lay on the rough wood floor gasping for air, a voice came to them out of the gloom. "Cousin Ginny, Cousin Finn, are you alright?"

Ginny and Finn stared up at the face peering down at them. A boy, who looked about their age, stared down at them with concern. Suddenly the floor they were on started tilting sharply to one side, and they felt themselves start to slide. The boy fell onto his knees next to them.

"You two took quite a fall just now," he said, "are you injured?"

"No, we're fine," replied Finn warily, "Thanks for asking." He had no idea what was going on, but he didn't want to say anything until he had figured it out.

Just then, the room tilted sharply again and they could hear the sounds around them of people crying and calling for mercy. The air was stuffy and smelled faintly of vomit. Ginny scrunched up her nose and looked at the boy who was kneeling in front of them.

"We're on a ship, aren't we?" She asked. The boy looked at her in astonishment.

"You don't know where you are? You must have hit your head or something. I'm going to get Mother." He disappeared into the gloom.

Finn and Ginny looked at each other. Finn suddenly thought of the remote and went to hide it in Ginny's fanny pack, when he realized that she wasn't wearing it. In fact, she wasn't wearing anything that she had left home in. Her jeans and tee-shirt had been replaced with a blue dress and white bonnet! Ginny found that there was a bag tied around her waist that she quickly hid the remote in.

Ginny looked down at herself and then at Finn and exclaimed, "Finn, you have short pants on!" Finn looked down and saw that his jeans had been replaced with a short pair of pants that stopped at his knees. He was also wearing long stockings and leather shoes.

"How did this happen?" he whispered. "And where are our backpacks?" Both twins started looking frantically around them, but their backpacks were gone. Everything that they had so carefully packed had disappeared.

Just then, the boy came back with his mother. She had auburn hair and a face made for smiling.

"I hear you two took a tumble...." And that was when the world went crazy. The ship started rocking even harder, people were calling out in fear, and a huge sound like a shot cracked through the dark.

"What was that?" Ginny asked her eyes wide.

"I don't know," replied the woman, looking a little frightened.

At that moment a man screamed, "We're sinking," and rushed by them to run up a nearby ladder. As he opened the hatch at the top of the ladder, a huge wave of water washed through it and knocked him down the ladder to the rough wooden planks below. Two men rushed over to help him, while another grabbed the hatch and closed it. One of the men said, "Hush now; you're frightening the women and children. God will look after us."

Finn looked at Ginny excitedly "Ginny, I know where we are! It's the year 1620, and we're on the Mayflower!"

"Of course you're on the Mayflower, you silly boy," exclaimed the woman, "You've been on it since we boarded in Southampton in August. It's been over two months we've been trapped on board this ship. Don't tell me you've hit your head and forgotten?" She looked at him worriedly.

"Ah, no...Aunt... (at least he hoped that's what she was since the boy had called them cousins)...I remember now...you're right though, I must have hit my head a bit," said Finn.

"Well, perhaps you should both go to bed now," she said as she pointed to a small wooden bunk. "You're sure to feel better in the morning, and maybe by then this storm will have let up." Finn and Ginny obediently crawled into the bed and were surprised when the boy crawled in next to them. It seemed that they weren't going to have much privacy to discuss their situation.

Ginny's last drowsy thought to herself as she drifted off to sleep was "At least I know that the ship's not going to sink; otherwise the Pilgrims would have never landed in Plymouth."

4

A New Day

The next morning, the boy was gone, the ship had stopped its violent rocking, and Ginny and Finn were alone in the bunk.

"What did she mean we've been on board ship for over two months?" Surely it didn't take the Pilgrims that long to get to America?" asked Ginny.

"I think I remember reading that they had lots of delays in England and weren't allowed to leave the ship while they waited," Finn replied.

"Well, I'm glad that we didn't get here earlier then, this place is claustrophobic!"

"That should make it easier to find Mom and Dad if they're here," replied Finn.

"You're right; we should start looking for them right away! Wouldn't it be great if they were on this ship?" Ginny said excitedly as she started to climb out of the bunk.

"Wait," cautioned Finn, "we need to talk, and I don't think we're going to get many chances here. Remember what Uncle Peter said about the remote?"

"That's right; a number should appear in the screen telling us how many days we have to stay here." Ginny pulled the remote out of the bag around her waist. She stared down at it in horror. "Finn, it says we have to stay here three hundred and ninety-five days, more than a whole year! Uncle Peter never said it could take that long!"

"Remember though, in our time it will only be a few minutes, so we won't be missing anything."

"Yes, but it's going to be more than a whole year *here*, and I don't think the Pilgrims had a very easy time of it."

"Just think of it as an adventure; the adventure of a lifetime. How many people do you know who can actually say they've met Pilgrims and seen our country right at its beginning?"

Ginny sat and thought for a minute and then looked up at her brother. "You're right, it is an incredible adventure. I just freaked out for a minute; I'll be fine."

"That's my Ginny." Finn smiled. "Since we can't do anything about it, we might as well try to enjoy ourselves."

At that moment, their newly discovered Aunt, whom they were to later learn was named Aunt Eleanor, poked her head around the corner of the tiny bunk. "Time to get up you laz-a-bones," she said. "How are you two feeling today?"

"Much better now, thank-you for asking," Ginny replied. She and Finn scrambled out of bed and followed Aunt Eleanor to one end of the ship, where a group of women were passing out bowls with what looked like oatmeal inside them. "Porridge," thought Ginny to herself, "that must be porridge."

Aunt Eleanor turned back to look at them, "The ship has stopped rocking, so the captain has given us permission to cook a hot meal."

"Makes a change from sea biscuits and cold beans," piped up a voice, and they turned to see the boy from the night before peering up at them from a corner. He was sitting next to another boy who looked a couple of years older. They were sharing a bowl, scooping porridge into their mouths with small wooden spoons.

Finn and Ginny sat down next to the two boys, holding their own shared bowl between them as they ate. Ginny wrinkled her nose at Finn as she took her first bite. The porridge didn't have any milk or sugar in it and tasted very bland. Finn didn't mind, and he ended up eating his share and most of hers. Back home, Aunt Martha always said that Finn must have a hollow leg that needed filling since he ate so much. Ginny blinked back the sudden tears that this thought brought. How was she ever going to stand living in these cramped quarters, not to mention being away from Aunt Martha, Uncle Peter, and her friends for a whole year?! Oh if only her parents were on this ship! She eagerly looked around as she ate, but she only saw unfamiliar faces; lots of them. She turned to the boys "How many people are on board this ship?" she asked.

The two boys looked at her strangely. "Don't you know by now?" one answered. "There's one hundred and two passengers plus the crew on board."

"No wonder it's so crowded," Ginny thought.

Across the room Aunt Eleanor nodded at the older boy and said, "John, take Francis and go tidy the bunks. Finn and Ginny, you can help wash the bowls."

Finn and Ginny looked at each other. Now at least they knew the names of their two new cousins. As the day went on, they learned some more of the Pilgrim's names. Most importantly they learned that their new uncle was named John. He was fairly tall compared to some of the other pilgrims, with a good-humored grin and a sharp wit. Finn liked him immediately, but he could see that there was at least one man on board, Captain Miles Standish, who did not like his new uncle. While his uncle entertained the other men with funny stories, Captain Standish sat in a corner brooding.

Finn turned to Francis and whispered, "What's up with him anyway?"

Francis answered, "He's often like that, haven't you noticed before? He and Father just don't get along well."

Just then the ship's master, Captain Jones, came down the ladder from the top deck with the ship's carpenter and some of the pilgrim leaders. They all had serious looks on their faces as they walked toward one of the main beams of the ship.

"What's going on?" whispered Ginny.

"Do you remember that huge cracking noise we heard last night?" Francis replied. "That beam over there cracked and now it's bending. It's one of the main beams that hold up the mast. They're afraid that the whole thing will break and the ship could sink or something. I hear there's even some talk of our going back to England!" The children sidled over to where the men were talking.

"Many of the crew want to turn back," said the carpenter. "This beam could go at any time and then we're all done for."

"Is there anything you can do to fix it?" asked the captain.

"Yes, please try," said William Brewster, one of the pilgrim leaders. "We can't turn back now. We have no homes to go back to. We've sold everything to make this voyage!"

"William, what about that large screw we brought on board?" said another of the pilgrims, "Could we use that to hold it up?"

"That just might work!" said the carpenter. "Where is it?"

The men went down a ladder to the lower cargo hold, with the children following discreetly behind. There they saw a dark, damp room packed full of barrels, wooden chests, items covered in canvas, and..."Oh yuck, there's a rat," said Ginny, and the children retreated back to their own deck.

After a bit the men came back carrying a big iron screw that they set up on blocks under the beam. That was when Finn understood what they were doing.

"It's just like jacking up a car," he said under his breath to Ginny. As the men turned the screw, it slowly pushed the cracked beam back in place. The pilgrims let out a collective sigh of relief. They wouldn't be forced back to England after all they had gone through to get this far.

5

More Storms

The men had fixed the cracked beam just in time, for the following day another storm came crashing in. This one seemed to last forever, especially for Ginny, who soon discovered that she was prone to getting seasick. One afternoon Finn poked his head into the bunk where she was laying in misery.

"Hey Sis, how are you feeling," he asked worriedly.

Ginny smiled up at him weakly. "I'll be fine; this can't last forever."

"I've checked the whole ship from top to bottom and Mom and Dad are definitely not on board," Finn said.

"So I'm sick and miserable for nothing," groused Ginny. "How come I get seasick and you don't? We're twins after all!"

Aunt Eleanor came bustling over. "No one knows why some people get seasick and others don't." She turned to Finn, "Don't worry, I'll take good care of her!" she said as she waved him away.

Finn wandered over to a corner where John and Francis were sitting and talking.

"Hey Finn," said John, "Want to see what it's like on the top deck in a storm?"

"Anything's better than sitting here any longer. I'd love to feel a fresh breeze on my face," Finn replied.

The three boys glanced around them and when they were sure no one was looking, climbed up the ladder to the upper deck, and pushed open the hatch. Finn poked his head up through the hole and gasped in surprise. The biggest wave he'd ever seen seemed to be coming right at him. He thought for sure they were going to capsize.

Francis pushed his head up next to him and yelled out "Look out John!" That was when Finn noticed John Howland, a servant to one of the passengers, standing next to a railing, just as the wave hit. John was flung into the sea from the force of the wave. Both Finn and Francis surged up the ladder yelling, "Man Overboard!" Just then another wave hit, and Finn felt himself sliding toward the edge of the ship. Suddenly the ship tipped sideways and Finn was flying through the air. He crashed into the freezing cold water and gasped for breath. As the wave raised him up he saw John Howland struggling in the water a few feet away.

"Good thing Mom signed us up for Junior Lifesaving," he thought as he grabbed John in a rescue hold.

"Finn, grab the rope," he heard Francis yell. Frantically he looked around and finally saw a rope in the water about ten feet away. He swam as hard as he could toward it and grabbed it just as another huge wave crashed down on them. He lost his hold on John, but John had also seen the rope and was able to grab onto it. Both of them hung on to the rope as hard as they could while the force of the wave pushed down on them. Just as he thought he couldn't hold his breath any longer, Finn could feel the rope jerking upward. He and John clung to the rope as the crew grabbed them with boat hooks and hauled them into the boat. While they were laid out on the deck gasping for air, Captain Jones came over and frowned down on them.

"What are you two doing up on deck? Don't you know by now that it's dangerous up here in a storm? Get down below, right now!" He glanced over to where Francis and John were standing off to the side, "And that goes for you too!" The four of them slunk off down the ladder to the lower deck.

"You saved my life!" John Howland said to Finn. "I thank you."

"It was nothing; you would have done the same for me," Finn smiled back.

John grinned at Finn and clapped him on the back. "No I wouldn't have; I can't swim!"

As Finn walked back to their bunk to change into dry clothes, he realized something. This was not just a fun game or vacation. He and Ginny could actually die here in the past.

6

New Friends

"Would you like to come and sew with us?" Ginny squinted up at the pretty young girl speaking above her. She felt weak, but not nauseous, for the first time in days.

"Yes, I think I would like that," she said as she struggled out of the bunk. The young girl's name was Mary Chilton and she was thirteen, a year older than Ginny and Finn. She chattered happily as the girls walked over to where a group of women were sitting in a circle sewing.

"Look everyone, Ginny is feeling better now!"

Aunt Eleanor smiled as she handed Ginny a bonnet to mend. "I'm glad that you've recovered Ginny."

"Thank you for taking such good care of me," Ginny replied as she reached down to give Aunt Eleanor a quick hug. "I don't know what I would have done without you."

Ginny settled down on the floor and listened as the women chatted away while they stitched. She was surprised to see the colors of the fabrics that they were working on. She had always thought that the pilgrims only wore dark clothing, but now she realized that wasn't true. She hadn't noticed it before, but as she looked around her, she saw that the pilgrims were wearing clothing of many different colors, much like in her own time.

Just then the group of women burst out laughing over some joke or other and Ginny realized something else; that the pilgrims weren't the serious, unfriendly people she had imagined them to be. Both the women and men laughed and joked with each other, and about twenty feet away she could see a number of men playing a game that looked rather like horseshoes; they were throwing a circle made of rope over a wooden stake that they had set up.

Finn was over with the men and boys who were playing Quoits, the name of the horseshoe-like game. As he laughed with the rest when the ship rolled and made him miss his shot, he realized that he was becoming fond of the pilgrims he had met on this voyage; they were starting to feel like friends and family. He admired how they ignored the hardships of the ship; living in such close quarters with little fresh air or hot food without complaining, and he liked how they treated others with respect, even some of the crew members who made fun of them or taunted them for their beliefs.

Uncle John and Aunt Eleanor were considered "strangers," people who did not belong to the original band of religious separatists who had first planned the voyage. But they too had been kind, and Finn felt like they were his real Aunt and Uncle, though he supposed they were actually some sort of great-great grandparents or something. According to Uncle Peter, the families they would meet when they traveled back in time would be their own direct ancestors. He grinned to himself; that meant that either Francis or John might be some sort of great-great grandparent too!

"What are you grinning at?" Francis said as he punched Finn on the shoulder.

"Nothing much," Finn said as he punched back. "Just happy that the storms are over for now, and that we can have a hot meal!"

One of the men looked worriedly over at them. "Better enjoy what meals you can now boys, our food is running low, and we may have to start rationing even more soon."

Later, as Finn dipped his sea biscuit into the rich stew of the afternoon meal, he thought of the man's words. He was already hungry almost all of the time and couldn't imagine having even less food to eat. He was so hungry that he didn't even mind it when a maggot-like creature dropped out of his sea biscuit into the bowl, though he flicked it out and didn't eat it like he had seen some of the sailors do. He hadn't gotten that desperate for food, though he wondered if he soon would be.

7

The First Death

Finn, Ginny, wake up!" whispered Francis urgently, "William Button has died."

The twins looked up at him dazedly. "Wha...William is dead? But we thought he was getting better," cried Ginny. She and Mary had taken to visiting the sick boy to try and cheer him up, so his death took her especially hard.

"He took a turn for the worse in the middle of the night and passed away," said Francis. "He's with the Lord now. There will be a service for him up on deck this afternoon."

It was a sorrowful group of pilgrims who stood on the deck later that day listening to William Brewster pray. They had all come so far, and were so close to their goal. To lose one of their members now, after all they had gone through was difficult and didn't bode well for the future.

Then, as William's body slipped into the sea, Finn looked up and saw a bird fly by. He nudged Ginny, "Look, a seagull!"

Some of the crew members saw it and started pointing excitedly.

"Why are they so excited?" Ginny asked.

"It must mean that land is near!" Finn exclaimed.

Later that afternoon as they ate their meal, the passengers talked excitedly among themselves.

"Seagulls mean land is near for sure," said Stephen Hopkins, "Our journey is almost over, and now the real work will begin."

"Goodman Hopkins, you've been to the New World before," someone asked, "What are the Indians like?"

Stephen paused for a moment. "They are fearsome fighters. At Jamestown we couldn't go outside of the fort without being attacked. But that was partly our own fault; when they refused to trade with us, Captain Smith attacked them and stole their food. I think that if you treat them fairly, they will treat you fairly, but first you have to show them that you mean well, and that might be difficult."

William Brewster chimed in, "Yes, we are all scared of each other, both Indians and Europeans, so sometimes we attack out of fear. It is our hope that we can make peace with our new Indian neighbors and live in harmony with them. Plus, it is my understanding that the various tribes have been fighting with each other lately, so we will have to tread carefully until we figure out what is going on. Let us all pray for peace with our new neighbors."

"But do they want us to be their neighbors?" Finn exclaimed.

Everyone looked at him in surprise. "Rather too late to be asking that now!" Uncle John laughed. "We have no place left to go; we've given up everything to come here. Besides from what I heard before we left, many parts of the New World had some sort of plague, and most of the Indian population was killed. They say that one tribe used to have over eleven thousand men and now it only has about a hundred. There is a lot of vacant land out there that's just waiting to be farmed."

"Plague," Ginny said worriedly, "Could we catch it?"

"No, from what I hear it has ended. It's just like what happened in England when the plague spread there from Asia. It swept through the country and killed more than a third of the population. Then, for some unknown reason it stopped for a while."

"This is a cheerful conversation for a group of people who are finally going to be able to leave this ship soon," exclaimed Aunt Eleanor "Let's talk about something else, like how glad I'll be to wash our clothes!"

"Or about how good it will be to walk on ground that's not moving?"

"Or to not be cooped up in this dark room all day?"

As the others listed all of the things they were looking forward to, Ginny could only think of poor William Button, who would never be able to do those things again.

8

Land Ho!

Land Ho!" someone shouted, "Land Ho!" The passengers ran up to the top deck to see what was happening. It had been three days since William had died and they'd seen the seagull, and a very discouraging three days it had been with no land in sight. And now, there it was, miles and miles of green trees way off in the distance.

"And not a moment too soon," thought Ginny. "We're almost out of fresh water and food."

Both she and Finn had lost so many pounds that they were starting to look like walking skeletons. Food had become an obsession with them, and they would often spend the evenings quietly planning the huge feast they would have when they finally returned home. Finn wanted steak and home fries, while Ginny wanted turkey and stuffing. They'd decided to have both. But that was still months in the future, and Ginny knew there were more hard times to get through. For now though, it was just a huge relief to know that they would soon be able to leave the ship. Ginny, along with many of the other passengers, stood at the rails, drinking in the sight of land.

The ship eventually turned toward the south, following the coast down toward where they had permission from King James to settle. Finn came and stood alongside Ginny at the rail.

"So this is what our country looked like before the Europeans came," he said.

"It's so beautiful," replied Ginny. "But a bit scary too. After all of this time on board ship I can hardly wait to get off it, but when we land, there will be no one to welcome us, no place to buy food, and no hotels or homes to stay in. There are no hospitals to go to for help, no army to protect us. We're completely on our own. And I'm not sure that all of these people really know what they are doing! They are here because they have no place else to go, not because they are great explorers or adventurers. They're really just a group of regular people."

"Regular people with a lot of strength and determination though," said Finn.

Ginny looked up at him and smiled. "You always know what to say to make me feel better."

Just then the crew shouted for the passengers to get below. In front of them were huge waves breaking on some rocks. The crew rushed around adjusting the sails and looking for submerged rocks as the passengers went back into the dark, damp lower deck. As they sat huddled in the dark room, it felt even more unbearable than usual after being so close to land. One of the pilgrims started singing a hymn and the rest joined in. Later, they could feel the ship turning around and heading back up the coast. The ship's captain and the Pilgrim leaders had decided to head back to a harbor they had spotted before they headed south.

Soon after that, the arguing began. Finn noticed a group of "Strangers," men like his Uncle John, off in a corner having a spirited discussion. The Strangers were not part of the group of religious Separatists who had organized this voyage. The Separatists had come to America to start a new life where they didn't have to worry about being thrown in jail or otherwise persecuted for their religious beliefs. The Strangers, like Uncle John, had also come to start a new life, but their reasons had more to do with wanting to make a better life for themselves. Finn quietly walked over to where Francis was standing near the men.

"What's going on?" he whispered to Francis.

"The storms blew us off course, and we don't have the supplies or time to find the place we were supposed to land. The leaders have decided to build our settlement here, but it's not where the king gave us permission to settle. Some of the men like my Father say that means that we don't have to do what the governor says, since he doesn't have permission to govern us here."

Stephen Hopkins spoke up. "Sirs, when I was shipwrecked on my previous voyage, the same thoughts came to me. But as time went on, I saw the error of my ways. We are all alone here in a vast and dangerous wilderness. We will need to stick together with common purpose if any of us are to survive."

Just then John Carver and William Brewster joined the men. "Gentlemen, Master Hopkins speaks good sense. Let us come together for the common good. If we have no charter from the king, then let us make our own agreement amongst ourselves as to how we will be governed."

The gathered men were silent for a moment, and then one by one gave their assent. With that, Carver and Brewster sat down and started to write as some of the men made suggestions.

Finn turned excitedly to Ginny who had appeared next to him. "Ginny, they're writing the Mayflower Compact, we're actually watching them write the Mayflower Compact! I can't believe it! It's the oldest self-governing document in our country's history, and we are actually watching them write it!"

The following day they stopped in a harbor. When the anchor hit the water, the crew let up a loud cheer and the passengers got down on their knees and thanked God for their safe voyage. Shortly after that, the twins watched as one by one, the adult male passengers solemnly walked up and signed the document that would become such a large part of our history.

The Mayflower Compact

In ye name of God, Amen. We whose names are underwritten, the loyall subjects of our dread soveraigne Lord, King James, by ye grace of God, of Great Britaine, Franc, & Ireland king, defender of ye faith, &c., having undertaken, for ye glorie of God, and advancemente of ye Christian faith, and honour of our king & countrie, a voyage to plant ye first colonie in ye Northerne parts of Virgina, doe by these presents solemnly & mutualy in ye presence of God, and one of another, covenant & combine our selves togeather into a civill body politick, for our better ordering & preservation & furtherance of ye ends aforesaid; and by vertue hearof to enacte, constitute, and frame such just & equall lawes, ordinances, acts, constitutions, & offices, from time to time, as shall be thought most meet & convenient for ye generall good of ye Colonie, unto which we promise all due submission and obedience. In witnes wherof we have hereunder subscribed our names at Cap-Codd ye 11. of November, in ye year of ye raigne of our soveraigne lord, King James of England, France, & Ireland ye eighteenth, and of Scotland ye fiftie fourth. Ano: Dom. 1620"

9

Going Ashore

Two days later, Ginny and Finn were sitting in the ship's longboat, watching the shore get closer and closer.

"I can't wait to step on dry land again!" exclaimed Ginny.

"I'm sorry you didn't get to come with me to help gather firewood the other day," replied Finn.

"It's totally unfair that the women and girls weren't allowed ashore then," pouted Ginny.

"That's because we menfolk didn't want anything bad to happen to you poor weak women," Finn teased.

"They certainly haven't heard of women's lib yet, that's for sure," grumbled Ginny.

"I don't think they have time to even think about that kind of stuff. They're too busy just trying to survive. Besides, you really wouldn't have liked cutting firewood for hours. I have blisters on my blisters from it. It's not like you missed out on anything really fun."

Just then the boat scrapped bottom and there was a mad scramble as everyone climbed out. Ginny ran up onto the beach, stretched, and took a deep breath.

"My that smells good." She smiled as she turned to her new friend, Mary Chilton, who also took a deep breath.

"It sure smells better than the rotten-smelling air on the ship!" Mary exclaimed. "Though it has been a bit better since the menfolk brought back that juniper to burn. At least that smells sweet."

Both girls smiled at each other and just enjoyed the feeling of finally being on land again. But their moment of leisure didn't last for long. There was a mound of clothes to wash, and Aunt Eleanor started rounding up the women to get started.

Later, as the two girls knelt next to each other scrubbing clothes, Mary said, "I'm sure glad that you are on the Mayflower, Ginny. It's nice to have another girl to talk with. I really miss my sisters."

"You have sisters?" Ginny asked in astonishment. "Why aren't they here with the rest of your family?"

"They stayed back in Leiden. I'm the youngest, so my parents brought me with them."

Ginny looked at her in puzzlement. "Isn't Leiden in Holland? I thought you were from England."

Mary laughed. "I forgot that you aren't a Separatist like us and don't know our history. Our families fled from England to Holland about twelve years ago. The English government wanted us to worship in their church, but that was against our beliefs. The members of our congregation were getting thrown in jail, fined, and some of them even had their property taken from them because they did not believe in the English church. Finally it got so bad that they tried to escape from England on a ship, but the captain stole their money and betrayed them. All of their goods were taken from them and they were paraded through town to be stared at by the townspeople. A number of our leaders were thrown in jail at that time, but they later were released.

The second time they tried to escape England, some soldiers came when the ship was only half loaded. Most of the men were on board the ship and the Captain sailed off, leaving most of the women and children still on shore. None of the women knew what would happen to them. The English authorities didn't know what to do with them either; their husbands were on their way to Holland, and they had no homes to go back to. The authorities ended up letting the women and children go, and eventually everyone was together in Holland."

"But why did you all leave Holland then? Were they persecuting you there too?"

"No, the people were more tolerant in Holland, though it was hard for our parents to make a living there because they were newcomers. The only work they could find was very menial and difficult, and many of them were becoming ill from it. Also, Holland's treaty with Spain was about to expire, and they were afraid that there might be a war. Plus our parents didn't want their children to become Dutch or to be tempted by the ungodliness they saw around them."

"But to leave your sisters behind, to maybe never see them again, how could your parents do that?" Ginny immediately regretted her question when she saw Mary's eyes fill with tears.

"I hope someday that my sisters will come here to be with us. In the meantime, at least I have my parents with me."

Ginny stopped what she was doing and gave Mary a wet hug. "I'm sorry that I made you sad Mary."

"That's alright, it's not your fault," Mary said with a slight smile. "I don't want to think about all of that right now, I just want to think about how nice it is to be on land and away from the ship!"

* * * *

Later that evening, back on board the ship, Finn asked Ginny, "So how did you like your first day back on land?"

"It was wonderful! I am so sick of being on this ship....I didn't even mind washing clothes all day, though it was certainly a lot harder washing clothes by hand instead of using a washing machine. It really makes me appreciate how much easier it is to do things in the future. It took us all day to wash clothes! At home it takes barely any time at all!"

"Well I was helping the men who were putting the shallop back together."

"What's a shallop?" asked Ginny.

"It's a type of sailboat....you know....the one that's in pieces, the one that some folks slept in on the voyage over. It was damaged in all of the storms during the voyage, so they are trying to fix it, but that is going to take longer than they thought, so they are going to send out some men to do some exploring on foot. They need to find the best place to make their settlement before it gets too cold."

"And I suppose only men will be allowed to go, as usual."

"Well, men....and a boy..."

Ginny looked at him suspiciously. "What boy would that be? she asked.

Finn grinned sheepishly. "Actually that would be me. I guessed I impressed them with what a hard worker I am, so they're bringing me along to help haul water and stuff."

Ginny looked at him worriedly. "Finn, it's dangerous out there. Didn't you notice how the men were keeping guard the whole time we were on shore? I've been hearing stories about how the Indians have attacked and killed people in this area, plus there are wolves and who knows what other wild animals; way more than there are in modern times. I don't want you to go. What if something happens to you?" Ginny was practically crying.

Finn put his arm around her. "Ginny, everything is going to be o.k. I don't remember much about the story of the Pilgrims, but I'm pretty sure that no one died from an Indian attack, or from wolves. I'll be fine."

"I hadn't thought of that. I don't remember reading anything about that sort of thing either....I guess knowing that makes me feel a little better about it. I wish I could go with you though; I don't like us being separated." Then she brightened a bit, "But I am having fun getting to know Mary better. It's nice to have a girlfriend again."

Finn looked at her seriously. "Friends are nice, but I wish we had our parents back."

Ginny blinked back a quick rush of tears. "Don't worry, we'll find them. It just probably won't be on this trip."

10

Exploration!

Finn sat uncomfortably in the long boat as it headed toward shore. He, along with most of the passengers and crew, had gotten very sick shortly after their last trip ashore. They had all been so excited to eat their first fresh food in months that they gobbled down the mussels they had found clinging to the rocks without a second thought. Unfortunately, most of the folks who ate them got food poisoning. Being on board ship with over a hundred people, many of whom had either diarrhea or were vomiting (or both), was not an experience he ever wanted to repeat. He felt a lot better now, but was still a bit weak from his sickness, and he was uncomfortable in the borrowed quilted armor Aunt Eleanor had insisted that he wear. It wouldn't protect him as much as metal armor, but hopefully he wouldn't need it anyway. For once, Ginny did not envy him as he headed out in the boat with the exploration party. She was quite happy to stay on the ship this time and recover a bit more from the shellfish!

After a long wade through the water to get to the shore, Captain Miles Standish, the leader of the expedition, had them all walk single file along the sand. It was tough going walking on the sand with their armor and weapons, and Finn was glad that he wasn't wearing the heavy metal doublets that a few of the men had on.

Suddenly, the man in the front shouted—there were people up ahead! Thinking it was Captain Jones and some of his seamen who were also somewhere on shore, the group started waving their hands. Then Finn realized that they weren't Europeans; they were Indians, about six men, and a dog! The Indians turned and ran and the Pilgrims excitedly discussed what to do.

"We need to try and make contact with them," exclaimed Bradford. "We need to let them know that we mean them no harm, and would like to trade with them."

"We also need to be careful," cautioned Captain Standish. "They may be setting an ambush for us. We'll follow them, but everyone keep a close watch. They appear to be going in the same direction we were anyway, so we won't be losing time by following them."

Finn pinched himself...this had to be a dream. He was with a group of Pilgrims, following Indians down a beach. Boy, he wished he could tell some of his friends back home about his adventures!

Later, after slogging through the sand for what seemed like ten miles (but was most likely about seven), Finn realized that real adventures aren't at all like what he'd read about in books. They were long, tiring, hungry, and thirsty work. Night was starting to fall and they still hadn't caught up with the Indians or seen any sign of the river that they had been originally searching for. Finn wasn't sure if he could go on much longer, so he was very relieved when Captain Standish decided that it was time to make camp. Soon they had a roaring fire going and everyone felt better. They all had a bit of biscuit and cheese (which was all they had to eat) and sat by the fire trading stories. Stephen Hopkins told his tale of being shipwrecked on his way to Jamestown, and William Bradford told of the Pilgrim's difficulties in leaving England. Finally, sentries were posted, and Finn rolled himself into a blanket and fell into a deep sleep.

* * * *

"Wake-up boy!" Stephen Hopkins said as he shook Finn awake. Finn looked out from under his blanket.

"It's still dark out," he muttered.

"But the sun is about to come up, and we want to get started as soon as we can see the Indians' tracks."

Finn crawled out of bed and helped to break down the camp as the sun slowly lightened the sky. Soon they were marching on their way again.

Not too long after they started out, the Indians' tracks led into the woods where a creek flowed. Now the going got a lot rougher, with bushes tearing at their clothes and steep hills to climb up and down. Finn realized that yesterday's march, which he had thought so difficult, was actually pretty easy. After hiking about four hours without seeing any sign of human habitation, they discovered a deep valley with paths running through it. A deer bounded away before they could get a shot off at it. Fresh meat would have been good, but even better was the freshwater spring that the deer had been drinking from. Finn gratefully threw himself down for a drink. Never had water tasted so good!

After a brief rest, Captain Standish ordered everyone to march again, this time toward shore. "We can't afford to waste any more time trying to find the Indians. We need to go back and explore closer to shore," he said.

Later in the day Finn saw what looked like a path leading off into the woods. He nudged the man in front of him who was plodding along looking at the ground.

"Look at that, where do you think it goes?"

The man looked up and then called out, "Hey Captain! Finn found a path over here!"

Captain Standish came over and smiled at Finn. "Good eyes son. Let's go see what you've discovered." They all walked along the path until they came to some mounds of sand, one of which was covered in old mats.

"Goodman Hopkins, do you have any idea what these might be?"

"No Captain, I've never seen anything like it. Let's dig into them and see what we find. Finn, you discovered the path, go ahead and dig and see what is under there."

Finn took a stick and started digging into the soft sand. Soon he had uncovered an old, rotten bow and some arrows, and then said, "You know, I think I know what this might be; I think it's a burial mound!"

William Bradford looked worried. "You very well could be right Finn. In that case, I think we should cover it back up. We don't want to offend the Indians by digging up their graves. Let us continue along this path and see what else we can find. I think I see a field up ahead."

Sure enough, not much farther up the path was an old corn field and then an old broken down house that had a large metal kettle inside that looked like it came from a ship.

"How in the world would that get here?" asked Finn. "It looks like it must have come from Europe."

"Europeans have been trading with the Indians up and down this coast for over a century," replied Stephen. "That's how so many of them caught various European illnesses and died. Every time different groups of peoples come together for the first time, one of them seems to bring illness to the other. It's been happening in Europe for centuries. It's a horrible tragedy, but until we discover how to stop these illnesses, it's going to keep on happening."

Finn nodded. He was bursting to tell Stephen about how many of the old diseases were cured in the future, but knew that wouldn't be a good idea. Just then, one of the other men pointed to another mound of sand. This one looked different from the burial mound that they had seen earlier. Captain Standish ordered some men to dig into it to see what it might be. They soon uncovered a small basket full of corn seed, and as they kept digging, they uncovered even more. Finn stared at it. Corn. He was practically salivating he was so hungry. They had been cutting back on the food rations more and more as the leaders realized that they did not have enough food to get through the winter.

Captain Standish and William Bradford looked at each other. "If we take it, we'll be stealing from our new neighbors," said Bradford.

"But if we don't, we may starve to death. We have no idea how the seeds we brought will grow in this land. If they fail, we will surely all starve to death. We don't have enough food to risk that," replied Captain Standish. "We're practically starving already, and the winter has just started. There is no way we can survive if our crops fail next summer."

"If we take it, we will need to repay them as soon as we can," Bradford said thoughtfully. "We must make contact with them and pay them back."

After more discussion, the group decided to fill the kettle and their pockets with as much corn as they could carry, and then give the kettle back and repay the Indians for the corn, once they discovered who it belonged to.

With that, the tired group marched back to a large freshwater pond that they had discovered earlier. By that time it was raining, so even the large fire they built didn't offer much comfort. It was a cold, miserable group of men who set out the next morning.

* * * *

"Hey Captain, I think we've passed this rock before," yelled one of the men.

Finn looked at the boulder and he knew that they were lost. They had definitely walked by it already once.

Most of the Pilgrims were town-dwellers and had no experience in the woods, so of course they would get lost, Finn thought glumly. As if to emphasize this thought, suddenly, right in front of him, William Bradford's leg pulled out from under him and he fell over.

"Whoa!" yelled Finn, "What happened?"

Stephen and the other men in front were laughing as Bradford looked at his leg in astonishment.

"You just got caught in a deer snare Master Bradford," laughed Stephen as he helped Bradford get untangled.

"How ingenious," Bradford said as he examined the snare. "Perhaps we could use one of these to catch a deer. We certainly haven't had much luck shooting them!"

Eventually the weary marchers made it back to the beach after slogging through a swamp with water up to their knees. It was with great relief that they spotted the Mayflower and shot off their muskets in greeting.

11

Francis Gets Into Trouble

For the next few days Finn was happy to stay on board the Mayflower and rest from his adventures. Soon another exploring expedition was sent out, but Finn wasn't selected to go along this time. He didn't feel too badly about that, since one of the purposes of the expedition was to collect more of the buried corn that they had discovered. He understood why the Pilgrim leaders made this decision, but he was still uncomfortable with it. The unexpected delays in leaving England had depleted the Pilgrim's food supplies, and even though they were rationing, food was getting scarce. The leaders were responsible for keeping everyone alive, and the corn that they had discovered could make the difference between life and death. Finn knew that if he was the one responsible for keeping everyone alive, that he might even make the same decision; especially with so many young children on board. Yet he also still felt a bit guilty about taking the Indians' corn. He did feel better when he heard the Pilgrim leaders assure everyone that they intended on paying the Indians for the corn, but they still had to figure out who owned it.

Being cooped up on the Mayflower was slowly getting on everyone's nerves. People were starting to get short-tempered with each other, and the boys especially were feeling the confinement.

One day Francis came up to Finn and asked, "Finn would you like to make some squibs?"

"What's a squib?"

"You take some black powder and pour it into the shaft of a duck feather. They sometimes use them to light the cannons."

"And it's o.k. if we make them?" asked Finn, "It sounds a bit dangerous."

Francis looked at him in surprise, "Of course we can," he said. "My dad showed me how."

The two boys went to the tiny room where Uncle John and Aunt Eleanor slept, and Francis showed Finn how to make squibs. Leaning against the wall was Uncle John's musket.

"Want me to show you how to shoot a musket?" asked Francis.

Finn, thinking that Francis was talking about doing this when they were on land, said, "Sure," and turned back to the squib he was making. When he looked up again, Francis had a burning stick in his hand and was lighting the wick of the musket.

Finn's eyes got wide and his heart started racing. "What do you think you're doing?! he yelled. "There's black powder in here!" But it was too late. Francis fired off the musket which ignited some of the powder on the floor that had spilled from the powder barrel. Some of the adult passengers had heard the musket shot and Finn's warning yell, and they came running with water buckets to help put out the fire. Luckily, they were able to stop the fire before it spread, but it was a near thing.

Later that evening, when Uncle John came back from the wood-gathering expedition he had been on, he called both boys into his cabin and looked at them sternly.

"Explain yourselves."

Francis spoke up. "It's not Finn's fault. I'm the one who shot off the musket. He didn't even know I was going to do it."

"What were you two even doing playing with the black powder in the first place?" Uncle John demanded.

"We were making squibs, just like you showed me," said Francis.

"When I showed you how, I also told you not to make them unless I was around. You disobeyed me Francis. I am very disappointed in you."

Finn glanced at Francis in surprise. Francis refused to meet his eyes. "Yes Father, I was wrong. And I led Finn into trouble too. I told him you said it was alright to make the squibs."

Uncle John looked down at Francis. "Son, I am proud of you for owning up to what you've done, but I'm still going to have to punish you for disobeying me."

Francis continued to look at his feet. "Yes Father."

Uncle John looked over at Finn. "Finn, I had thought you had more common sense than this. Playing with black powder is very dangerous. I hope you've learned your lesson. Now leave the room while I give Francis his whipping."

Glumly Finn left the tiny room and walked over to where Ginny was sitting with her friend Mary.

"What happened?" whispered Ginny.

"I was really stupid. I should have known that Uncle John didn't want us playing with the black powder."

"How were you to know?" Ginny defended him stoutly. "Things are so different here than they are at home. Kids do all kinds of things here that they don't do in our time. Have you noticed how much more responsibility kids have here? They are like little adults, helping with almost all of the chores."

"Yes, that's why I thought it might be o.k." said Finn. "I thought we were making the squibs to help light the cannons or something."

Suddenly both children realized that they had forgotten that Mary was next to them. "What do you mean, 'in your time?'" she asked, puzzled.

Ginny and Finn looked at each other in dismay. "I just meant the town we come from." said Ginny. "In our town the kids don't help out as much as they do here."

"Why not?' asked Mary. "Don't they want to help their families?"

"I'm not sure why they don't" replied Ginny. "Maybe it's because their parents don't expect them to help."

"I like helping out my parents," said Mary. It makes me feel good to be able to help them since they've done so much for me."

Ginny looked sadly at Finn. "I wish I had helped Mom and Dad around the house more when I had the chance."

"Me too," said Finn glumly, "Me too."

12

Another Expedition

It was now early December and the weather was getting colder. The Pilgrims still had not found a suitable place for a settlement, and their leaders decided to send yet another expedition out, this time in the repaired shallop, to make one last exploration of the bay that they were anchored in.[1] Finn was excited that he was again selected to go along on this expedition. He was getting very tired of the Mayflower, and felt that if he had to spend another day on it he would start screaming. He was used to being outdoors all of the time at his aunt and uncle's cabin and

---

[1] Cape Cod

really didn't like being cooped up inside the ship for so long.

Finn was so happy to be off the ship that he didn't even mind the cold wind that froze the sea spray on their coats so that all of the men in the shallop looked like ice statues. Two of the men were sick and were coughing and hacking. Still, Finn was happy. Anything was better than the cramped quarters of the Mayflower.

Toward evening they rounded a bend and in the far distance saw about ten Indians on shore gathered around a large black object. One of them spotted the shallop and they all started scurrying around gathering up their things before they ran off into the woods.

"What do you think they were doing?" asked Bradford.

"I don't know, but why don't we land for the night and we can take a look tomorrow," replied Hopkins. "We need to stop for the night anyhow, so it might as well be here."

This turned out to be easier said than done as the bay was very shallow and it was hard to find a way to get to shore. Once they finally landed, Captain Standish set some of them to building a barricade of logs, sticks, and pine boughs for protection and to block the wind, while others gathered firewood. Soon there was a roaring fire going, which was a great comfort after the cold and windy day.

* * * *

The next morning they decided that some of the men would take the shallop and continue exploring the shoreline, while others would walk along shore and see if they could spot any good sources of fresh water or places to build a settlement. Finn was with the land expedition and as they were walking, he spotted a large lump in the sand.

"That looks like what the Indians were looking at when we saw them," he exclaimed.

As they got closer Stephen said, "It's a Grampus."

"Looks like some type of whale," thought Finn. "It must have beached itself."

"Look over there, that's where the Indians were," said Bradford. "And there is another Grampus."

The small group of Pilgrims trudged along the sand to where they had seen the Indians the afternoon before. This Grampus had long thin strips sliced out of it, which must have been what the Indians were working on when the Pilgrims spotted them.

"Here's the Indians' trail," said Stephen. "Shall we follow it and see if we can make contact?"

They all agreed to follow the trail to see what they could find. The trail went along the shoreline for a while, but then it veered off into the woods. As they followed it, Finn reflected again on what an amazing adventure he was on. He took a deep breath of the cool, clean forest air and marveled at where he was and what he was doing. Not long after, they came to some signs of inhabitation: a large graveyard, abandoned houses and old corn fields. After walking through the forest for hours, the group never came upon a live person. By the end of the day they were all hungry and exhausted. Finn, who was used to three meals a day, was finding it especially hard to hike so long without food. He was very glad when they got back to shore and saw the shallop not too far off. He helped to build another barricade and gather firewood, and then had a watery stew for supper. After that, he fell into a fitful sleep.

* * * *

A loud cry split the air and Finn woke with his heart pounding. It was still dark outside, and the sentinel was yelling, "To Arms! To Arms!" The men around him quickly grabbed their muskets and let off a few shots into the night. Then all was silent. The men looked at each other uneasily.

"I think I've heard that sound before," said one of the sailors who had come on the expedition. "I believe it is wolves or foxes."

"We'll put some extra men on watch the rest of the night, just in case," replied Captain Standish. "We don't want to take any chances."

As everyone settled down again, Finn found it hard to get back to sleep. He wasn't sure exactly what wolf howls sounded like, but he didn't think it sounded like the noise that had woken him up. Something just didn't feel right about it. It was just before dawn when he finally fell asleep, only to be woken up almost at once by the men stirring and getting ready to leave. After a group prayer, they had a quick breakfast and started to carry things down to the shallop.

Finn was up by the barricade grabbing a load to bring down to the shallop when a loud cry split the air again. At the same time, one of the men came running up; screaming, "They are men.... Indians, Indians!"

Then things started happening very fast-- arrows were flying through the air. Captain Standish pushed Finn behind him--protecting him from the arrows--and fired a shot in the direction of the yelling. Another man also fired a shot off. Men were running to grab their muskets. There were now four men with muskets at the barricade, while others were still down at the shallop. As Finn crouched down behind the shooting men, he heard one of the men at the shallop calling for a firebrand to light his musket. Finn was horrified; how could the men at the shallop defend themselves without a way to light their muskets? Without even thinking, he rushed out, grabbed a log, and ran with it down to the shallop, dodging arrows as he went. All around him he could hear the strange war-cries of the Indians. He slid behind the shallop like a runner sliding into base, and handed the burning log to one of the men. Then he crouched panting for breath and shivering in reaction to what he had just done. Suddenly, one of the Indians gave a loud cry and the Indians all started running toward the woods.

Captain Standish yelled, "I want six men to stay at the shallop to guard it, and the rest come with me. I want them to know that we are not afraid of them."

Finn stayed with the men at the shallop and slowly got his breath back. Stephen Hopkins was standing next to him.

"Master Hopkins, why did the Indians attack us?" asked Finn. "We meant them no harm."

"Who knows?" replied Stephen. "It might be because we took their corn, though killing us for that seems a bit excessive. It might be because of something other Europeans who were here before us did. Unless we can actually make contact with them and talk with them, we might never know."

Just then Captain Standish and the rest of the men came back and did a head count. It appeared that no one, Pilgrim or Indian, had been hurt or killed, so perhaps there was still hope that they could somehow make peace with the natives. Finn went around gathering up all the arrows he could find. Some of the coats that had been hanging from the barricade were completely shot up with arrows. He marveled that in spite of all of the arrows and musket balls flying around, no one had been hurt.

They took off in the shallop soon after and continued exploring the coastline, going toward a harbor that one of the men from the Mayflower, Master Coppin, remembered from a previous voyage. The weather slowly got worse and worse. Finn could hear Edward Tilley, one of the sick men, coughing away. This weather was certainly not good for a sick man to be out in. It started raining and snowing, and the seas started getting very rough. Suddenly one of the sailors gave out a yell—the rudder had broken! With no way to steer it, the shallop started to flounder. Two of the men grabbed oars and used them to steer with, but the weather wind and waves got stronger and taller. Icy water was washing over the men and the boat rose up and crashed down in each wave.

Master Coppin called out, "Be of good cheer men! I see the harbor ahead...we're going to make it!" Just then, as if to contradict his words, the mast broke and fell to the deck. During the confusion of clearing off the broken mast and sails, Master Coppin suddenly cried out again, "Lord be merciful unto us; I have never seen this place before." Instead of the calm harbor they thought they were going to, there were waves breaking on rocks right in front of them!

Master Coppin called out, "We have no choice, steer toward the rocks and run aground!"

One of the other sailors called out, "No men; be of good cheer! Row, row hard away from the rocks, we can get past this!" Everyone who was able grabbed an oar and rowed as hard as they could. The rain grew heavier, the world grew darker, yet still they rowed. Finally, after what seemed like forever, they could feel a difference in the wind and waves. They were on the lee side of what they would later discover was an island. After some discussion, it was decided to land the boat, even though some of the men were afraid of being attacked by Indians again. Everything and everyone was soaking wet. A fire was a necessity, so as soon as they landed they started the wearying job of searching for dry firewood. Once the comforting fire was started, everyone felt better, even though it continued to rain all night.

* * * *

The next day was bright and full of sunshine. After exploring the island[2] that they found themselves on, the men realized that on the other side

---

[2] They named it "Clark's Island" after the first of them to step on its shores.

of the island was a harbor that might just be what they were looking for in a settlement. After spending two days on the island drying out, fixing the shallop, and just resting and recovering from their ordeal, they landed in what was to be their future home. The harbor was deep enough for the *Mayflower;* there were old unused cornfields, running streams, and no signs that Indians currently inhabited this land. Their long search was finally over, and the next day they returned to the *Mayflower* with the good news.

Map of Cape Cod and Plymouth Harbor

Adapted from "Woods New England Prospect,"
1858 Edition.

13

On Board Ship

While Finn was out on expedition, Ginny remained on the ship with the rest of the passengers. She too was tired of being cooped up on the Mayflower, but since she was a girl, she didn't have the option of getting off the ship with the men. So, as she watched Finn sail off in the shallop, she was feeling a bit resentful.

"Sometimes I wish I was a boy," she muttered to herself.

Mary, who was standing next to her, looked at her strangely. "Why ever would you want that?" she asked. "Those poor men have to go out in the cold, wet wind, while we get to stay here where it is warm. They will probably catch their death from it."

"Not Finn," Ginny said stoutly, "he never gets sick."

"No, not Finn," agreed Mary, "but maybe Edward Tilley. He was sounding really bad as they left, and this trip won't be good for him."

"I'm not sure this whole voyage is good for any of us," said Ginny thoughtfully. "Have you noticed how many people are getting sick lately?"

"I know, and poor Edward Thompson just died two days ago."

The two girls looked at each other. Unspoken, but on both their minds, was that Mary's father was also very sick. He was one of the oldest Mayflower passengers, and a few days ago he had taken to his bed with a high fever.

Just then the girls heard the sound of children crying, and they ran down to the lower passenger deck to see what the matter was. There they found three of the Moore children sobbing in the arms of Aunt Eleanor. Their brother Jasper had just died. He had only been about seven years old. Aunt Eleanor looked up at Ginny and Mary with tears in her eyes and Ginny could feel her own eyes filling with tears in response.

"There you are girls, we've been looking for you....Mary, your mother has been asking for you. I think she needs some help caring for your father. And Ginny, could you help me with these poor children?"

Ginny sat down and tried to help comfort the children, but she felt totally overwhelmed. All she could think of to do was to sing, so she held the children and sang and rocked until one of the women came over with some hot soup for them to eat.

* * * *

The next day Ginny woke up feeling fine, until she remembered the sadness of the day before. And things were about to get even worse. A few hours into the day it was discovered that William Bradford's wife Dorothy had fallen off of the ship and drowned. Master Bradford was still on the shallop with Finn and the other men, and everyone dreaded having to tell him that his wife had died. A gloom settled over the ship.

Aunt Eleanor's remedy for the depressing atmosphere was to keep busy. She gave the boys lots of chores to do and had Ginny go help Mary tend to her father. Mary's mother was looking exhausted from taking care of her sick husband, so Ginny and Mary helped her in any way they could: bringing the sick man food, cooling his forehead with damp cloths, or just sitting by him in case he needed something. All of their hard work and prayers didn't help though. Mary's father died the following day.

By the time Finn and the rest of the men from the expedition returned to the ship, Ginny was exhausted from sadness and worry, and when she saw Finn, she burst into tears in her brother's arms. She wasn't the only one crying as the men from the expedition soon heard of the deaths that had occurred while they were gone. Death was stalking the Mayflower passengers and he wasn't yet finished with them.

14

A New Home

A few days later, the Mayflower pulled into the harbor that was to be the Pilgrim's new home. Ginny was feeling much better now that that Finn was back on the ship and safe. The passengers were full of plans for their new settlement, and hope had returned to the Mayflower since the decision had been made to settle in the area that was known as Plymouth. After much discussion, it was decided to build their town on the mainland rather than on Clark's Island. There were old, unused corn fields on the mainland; a brook with fresh, sweet water; and a hill where they could place their cannons and defend themselves if they needed to. With this decision made, it was time to start building.

Once again, Finn was able to leave the Mayflower to work on land, while Ginny was left back on the boat with the women and children. However, this time Ginny didn't envy him. The weather had turned brutally cold and windy. Finn and the men on shore had planned on cutting trees for the settlement, but the weather was so bad that they could not get much done, and they ended up spending the night cold and wet with no shelter or food. Finn was miserable. He huddled as close to the fire as he could, trying to keep the rain off. What amazed him was the uncomplaining attitude of the men around him. In spite of all of the hardships that they had endured, they did not seem to have faltered in their resolve to build a new world for themselves and their families in this untamed land. As he dozed in and out of an uncomfortable sleep that night, Finn tried to imagine how his friends from the future and their families would handle the same situations that the Pilgrims had found themselves in. How would modern-day families, used to computers, TV, and all of the comforts of the modern world, deal with no food, no shelter, no electricity, and Indian attacks? It was hard to imagine.

The next day, the shallop managed to bring some food to the shore-party, but the weather was too rough to bring anyone back to the Mayflower, so they were forced to stay out in the cold and wind yet another day without shelter. The following day finally dawned clear. More men from the ship came to shore, and the work of building a settlement finally began in earnest.

Over the next few weeks the town was laid out, and the first building, the meeting house, was completed. Finn was surprised at how it was built. He had expected the Pilgrims to cut down logs and build a log cabin-style building, but that wasn't at all what they did. Instead, the building was put together more like modern-style buildings where the outer walls were framed with a series of uprights called studs. The space between the studs was woven with flexible sticks called "wattle," which was covered with a mixture of clay, earth, and grass called "daub." Then thin boards called clapboards were nailed to the outside walls to protect the clay walls from the elements. The thatched roofs were made with bundles of grass and reeds. Finn helped during all the stages of building. On the day it was finished, he stood in front of the meeting house and looked at it proudly. It was a fine, sturdy building and every time he looked at it, he felt a warm glow because he had helped build it--and not just build it, but build it from scratch. He'd helped cut down the trees, form the clapboards, gather the thatch, and worked on the actual building itself. And best of all, he now knew how it was done. Later, as he described the feeling to Ginny, he said, "I never knew that you could feel so good working hard like that. It was fun to learn how to build a house, but even better, I really feel like I've accomplished something."

Ginny smiled wanly back. She'd been working hard too, but her accomplishments had come at a high cost.

15

Hospital Ship

Finn was so excited about finishing the meeting house that Ginny didn't want to depress him with the tale of her time on the ship, so she didn't say much when they were able to meet that day. They hadn't seen each other for a few days, and she didn't want to spoil her time with him by talking about what was happening on the ship. Things weren't going well. More and more of the Pilgrims were getting sick, and the ship was starting to look more like a hospital than a working vessel.

The day after Finn's visit, Ginny woke up and started what had now become her daily routine. She and Mary visited the sick men and women:

bringing them food, wiping their faces with damp cloths, changing their bedding, or just doing whatever was needed most. Not only were the Pilgrims getting sick, but so was the ship's crew. One of the first people that Ginny and Mary brought food to that morning was a crew member. He was lying in his bunk sweating and coughing all alone. His shipmates had abandoned him out of fear of the sickness. As the girls walked over to his bunk, Mary suddenly went pale and tugged urgently at Ginny's arm.

"It's that man," she hissed in Ginny's ear.

Ginny was puzzled. "What man?" she asked.

"The crew member who was always cursing us and telling the captain that he should leave us and sail back to England. He's mean...I'm scared of him."

Ginny looked over at the sweat-soaked man. "He doesn't look so scary now, and Aunt Eleanor wouldn't have sent us to bring him some food if she thought he was dangerous. I know she's been feeding him for a few days now."

The girls edged cautiously over to the man and offered him some broth. He looked up at them gratefully and said, "I was wrong about you people. You show your love like true Christians...but we let one another lay and die like dogs. Thank you for your kindness to me." With that the girls relaxed some and helped him to sit up and eat his broth.

The girls' next visit was to the Fuller Family. As they entered the cramped room where Edward Fuller and his wife lay, they saw that they weren't the first ones there. Samuel Fuller, the Pilgrims self-educated doctor, was attending his brother. Doctor Fuller looked up as the girls walked in.

"Oh good, I could use some help just now. Could one of you girls hand me that bowl? I need to remove these leeches."

Ginny looked down in horror as Mary handed him the bowl. "What are you doing to him?" Ginny exclaimed.

"Why I'm bleeding him," replied the doctor. "Haven't you ever seen this done before?"

"No I haven't," Ginny replied firmly. "And I hope I never see it again!"

"But his humors are not balanced, and I need to do this to restore them," he said kindly. "I know it's not pretty-looking, but it's necessary." He smiled down at his patient. "We'll soon have you up and bustling about in no time brother."

As the girls left the room, Ginny whispered to Mary, "Mary, promise me if I ever get sick that you won't let him bleed me!"

Mary looked at her in surprise, "Why ever not? I've been bled before and it doesn't hurt.

"I don't care, just promise me," Ginny said furiously.

"But what if it could save your life?" asked Mary reasonably.

"Please, just promise me Mary!"

"If it means that much to you, I promise," said Mary, "But I think you're just being silly!"

Just then they heard the sounds of someone crying. They looked at each other in fear. Another passenger had died. In spite of all the hard work and effort the Pilgrims were putting into helping the sick passengers and crew, it seemed like the deaths were becoming more frequent, and the number of patients was increasing.

16

Lost in the Forest

Back on shore, Finn was cutting piles of reeds for the thatch roofs with some of the Pilgrim men. After working hard all morning, one of the men, John Goodman, turned to two of the others and said, "Why don't you two finish bundling up this pile while the rest of us start cutting those other reeds we saw?"

The men agreed, so John, Peter Brown, Finn, and the men's two dogs walked off into the woods toward the next meadow of reeds. After working hard gathering reeds for an hour or so, John, who was the oldest of the three, suggested that they stop for something to eat.

"Why don't we eat next to that lake we saw?" suggested Finn.

"Good idea," said John. "The dogs will enjoy that too."

Looking forward to a nice break by the lake, Finn and the two men started walking, but as they rounded the bend toward the lake, the dogs suddenly started barking wildly and bolted away. They had seen a deer way off in the distance and decided to give chase. Finn and the two men ran as fast as they could after them, and at first it was fun to be running through the woods, especially after bending over cutting reeds all day. After a while though, Finn was starting to get worried. It was taking way too long to catch the two dogs. When they finally did reach them, all three men were panting for breath.

"Boy, they led us on a merry chase!" exclaimed Peter.

"Too bad they didn't catch the deer," Finn said wistfully. "Venison steak would have been a nice change from all of the bird meat we've been eating."

"Men, I think we have a problem," interrupted John as he looked around the patch of forest they were in. I have no idea where we are, do you?"

That was when Finn realized that they had made a huge mistake. One of the first rules of survival in the woods is to pay attention to your surroundings. The three of them had been running so wildly, that none of them had noticed which way they were going. They were well and truly lost. Lost in a wilderness so vast that if they chose the wrong direction, they might never see another person again. Finn couldn't believe that he had been so stupid.

"Which way do you think we should go?" asked Peter.

"Let's go this way," John said as he pointed to the right.

"Wait," Finn said. "My dad...father once told me that if you are lost in the woods, the best thing to do is to stay put. That makes it easier for people to find you."

John thought about that for a moment, "It doesn't sit well with me to just sit here. How about this...Finn you stay here, and I'll walk as far as I can toward the right looking for something familiar. We'll stay within shouting distance, so that I can follow your voice back. Peter, you do the same thing, only go off toward the left. Maybe that way we can find a landmark that looks familiar or something."

The three agreed to try this, but after much searching, neither John nor Peter could figure out the way back to Plymouth. It was getting late, and night was coming. It was also starting to snow.

John looked worriedly around. "I think we need to stop for now and instead figure out how we're going to make it through the night. We still have our sickles; let's use them to make a shelter." With that the three got to work and soon had a rough shelter built. They huddled together with the dogs and finally ate the meal that they had gone down to the lake to eat.

That night was the worst of Finn's life. He was so cold that he was afraid that if he fell asleep he would never wake up again, so he and the others spent the night stomping their feet and moving their arms to keep the circulation going. When they weren't moving around they huddled together for warmth. Then, when it was pitch-black out, they heard a horrible howling.

"Lions!" said Peter with wide eyes, "It must be lions!"

"I think they are wolves," said Finn.

"Lions or wolves, whatever they are, it doesn't bode well for us," said John.

Just then, the two dogs started growling, and the men grabbed hold of their collars. None of them wanted another dog chase, especially with wolves around.

"We don't have any weapons, except for our sickles. I think our best chance is to try and climb a tree if the wolves get any closer."

They looked around for a likely tree, and once they found one, all three of them walked back and forth under it for the rest of the night, ready to leap into the tree if they spotted the wolves.

The next morning, as soon as there was light enough to see, they decided to start walking, since staying in the immediate area hadn't worked the day before. They walked and walked all morning. Finn was starting to despair. What would Ginny do here in this wilderness without him? And how would she explain what had happened when she got back to the future without him? He squared his shoulders. It wasn't like he was dead or anything. As long as he was alive there was hope. It was while he was thinking this that he noticed a tall hill up ahead.

"John, Peter, why don't we climb that hill and see if we can find the ocean?" he exclaimed.

The two men looked up, woken from their own gloomy thoughts. "Why you're right Finn," said John. "That hill looks high enough to see for miles around." With that, the three of them started climbing, and when they got to the top, they were able to see the bay and recognize two of the islands in it.

"That way, we need to go that way," pointed Finn with a huge grin. "We'll be home by dark!"

It was a cold, wet hike back. Finn's feet were so cold that they were going numb and felt like lead. He could tell by the trudging steps of the others that their feet were in as bad a shape as his. The hike back took a lot longer than they thought it would, but they finally made it. A shout went up when they were spotted, and soon they were surrounded by helping hands. John's feet had swollen so badly from the cold that his boots had to be cut off, and there was great concern that he would lose his feet, but eventually they healed. As Finn sat with a warm cup in his hand, Uncle John came over, squatted down, and gave him a big hug.

"You had us all very worried young man; especially your sister."

Finn looked at him with concern. "Where is she? Does she know that I'm back?"

Uncle John hesitated, "She was so worried about you that she insisted on coming to shore to help with the search party. While she was out in the woods looking for you, she suddenly cried out in pain and fell to the ground, like William Bradford did the other day. We took her to the meeting house, but she's still....."

Finn didn't wait for him to finish, he jumped up and rushed into the meeting house. There was Ginny, lying on a pallet.

"Hey sis, what happened to you?"

Ginny opened her eyes and looked up at him tiredly. "They told me you were safe, are you alright?"

"I'm fine, we just got lost for a while; I'm more worried about you. What's going on?"

"I don't know. I've been more and more tired lately, and then all of a sudden my legs just started hurting so bad...I don't know what's wrong...I just feel like sleeping all of the time....maybe I'm just tired" she said slowly as she drifted off to sleep again.

Finn suddenly felt exhausted himself. It had been a rough two days. He pulled up a pallet next to his sister, found some blankets, and fell into a dreamless sleep.

17

Fire!

"Finn, wake up! Get your sister and get out of here!" Finn abruptly awoke to find smoke swirling through the room. All around him men and women were jumping to their feet, grabbing the muskets, and running out the door. Quickly, Finn turned to Ginny, who was still asleep, and started shaking her.

"Ginny, get up, get up now!" But Ginny just mumbled in her sleep and turned over. Finn kept shaking and shaking her until finally she woke up. Then he grabbed her and pulled her toward the meeting house door. As he looked back at the room full of beds, he was horrified to see that William Bradford, who had been so ill a few days ago that they thought he might die, and John Carver were having trouble getting out of their beds.

"Quick, Masters Bradford and Carver need help!" He yelled as he got Ginny through the door. Immediately some of the men ran back into the burning building to rescue the Pilgrim leaders. Others were forming a bucket brigade to try and save the meeting house. Finn set Ginny down nearby and ran to help. The fire had started when a spark flew into the thatch roof, which had quickly caught fire. The rest of the building did not burn quite so easily, and after much work they were able to save it.

While he was happy that the building was saved, Finn was worried. Ginny just wasn't acting like her usual self. Normally, his sister would have wanted to help with the bucket brigade, but during the fire she just sat on a stump nearby staring listlessly into space. Once the fire was out, Finn led Ginny back to bed and made sure that she was comfortable. She immediately fell asleep, but Finn lay awake in bed worrying about her. Something just wasn't right.

* * * *

Over the next few weeks Finn and the rest of the colonists were kept busy re-thatching the meeting house, building a shed for their provisions, working on their houses, and helping the ill members of their party, whose numbers were growing ever larger. Finn had never worked so hard in his life. On top of all of this, it seemed like as soon as a job was completed, something would happen and they would have to start all over again. One day the thatch on another of the buildings caught on fire, and they had to completely re-thatch it. Another day it rained so hard that all of the newly plastered wattle and daub fell off. Mixed in with this was the constant fear of an Indian attack, and also fears of the wolves that sometimes prowled around the settlement. One man had to fend two of them off with a board as they tried to attack his dog.

And the number of deaths kept growing. In January eight people died. In February it was seventeen. Ginny wasn't getting any better, and now Aunt Eleanor, Francis, and John were sick too. Finn and Uncle John were exhausted from work and worry.

For weeks Ginny was so ill that she barely noticed the excitement over the various Indian sightings that were occurring more and more frequently: a group of twelve Indian men had been seen marching near the settlement; Captain Standish and Francis Cooke had left some tools out that had been subsequently stolen by some Indians; and one day two Indians had been spotted on a nearby hill, but ran away when Captain Standish and Stephen Hawkins went over to talk to them. All of these events caused great excitement and concern among the pilgrims, and whenever there was a sighting even the very sick men were roused up to help guard the settlement.

One day during this time Uncle John was sitting next to Aunt Eleanor holding her hand tightly and praying. Ginny was lying nearby and she could see tears forming under his closed eyes as he prayed for his wife and sons to live. Just then, Captain Standish marched up to the sitting man.

"Master Billington, you are late for guard duty! Leave here at once and take up your post!"

Uncle John ignored him and kept on praying.

"Master Billington, I am talking to you! Take up your post!"

Uncle John slowly stood up and looked down at the Captain. "Sir, you are a beggarly rascal to interrupt me when I am praying for my wife and children. Leave now, for if you disturb my wife or anyone in my family, I will beat the tar out of you!" The two men glared at each other; then Captain Standish turned on his heel and stomped off.

Uncle John sat down and winked at Ginny who was staring at him with wide eyes. "I probably shouldn't have done that, but that man would inspire a saint to murder, and I am certainly no saint. I suspect there will be trouble over this." He turned worriedly back to Aunt Eleanor who had slept through the whole confrontation.

Uncle John's words were prophetic. Captain Standish was not used to having any of the Pilgrims disobey his military orders, and he promptly had Uncle John dragged before the whole company where he was sentenced to have his neck and heels tied together. Uncle John begged for forgiveness, and it was decided that since this was his first offence that they would forgo the punishment. He immediately went back to his wife's bedside.

18

Illness

Things were getting worse and worse. More of the Pilgrims and seaman were coming down with fevers, strange aches and pains, and awful coughs. And even more people were dying. At one point there were only seven people who were well enough to care for the others. Finn didn't know why he wasn't getting sick like everyone else, especially since he spent day after day feeding, washing, and caring for the sick members of the group. Plus, he was dreadfully worried about Ginny. She just wasn't getting any better. Her legs were swollen and she was starting to vomit a lot. Half the time she didn't even seem to know that he was there. Aunt Eleanor and the boys were in the bed next to her, sick with the same mysterious illness, and Uncle John was beside himself with worry. Finn and Uncle John tried to help the patients as much as they could, bringing them cooling cloths for their foreheads, feeding them broth, or just holding their hands while they tossed and turned with fever. Samuel Fuller had suggested bleeding Ginny with leeches, but Finn had refused to let him. Fuller had walked away muttering, but he hadn't tried to force the issue. The bleeding hadn't seemed to help anyone else much anyway.

"Oh please Ginny, don't die...please don't leave me here by myself," Finn pleaded as he wiped her forehead.

Just then William Brewster walked in, "Finn, why don't you take a break for a bit? Captain Standish shot a goose and there is some hot stew on the fire that you could have. You aren't going to be able to help Ginny if you get sick yourself," he said kindly.

Finn slowly got to his feet as he wiped his eyes. "Thank-you sir, I think I will have some stew."

Finn got a bowl of stew and wandered away from the fire. If only he could do something to help Ginny and the others. But what? He didn't even know what they were sick with; there were so many different symptoms. He was so tired that he could barely think straight, but there was something tickling the back of his mind, some-thing he had read a while ago...if only he could remember what it was...Finn drifted off to sleep, too tired to even think anymore.

He woke up with a start. He'd been dreaming that he had figured out what was wrong with Ginny. Once again he felt like he almost had the answer, but it still eluded him.

"I guess I'll go back and bring Ginny some stew. She needs to get some food in her," he thought. He went over to the cooking pot, filled the bowl up with stew, and brought it over to where Ginny was lying. As he spooned some stew into her mouth, he noticed that her gums were strangely discolored. He peered closer at them, and a thought hit him like a hammer. He shouted out "Scurvy! You have scurvy!"

Samuel Fuller looked over at him in surprise. "Scurvy, what's that?"

"I remember reading about it awhile back; one of the symptoms is discolored gums and loose teeth. All we need to do is to give them some fresh fruit and they will get better," Finn said excitedly.

Samuel looked at him skeptically. "Fresh fruit, and where will we find that at this time of year?"

"I don't know, but I'm going to try," said Finn with determination as he ran out the door.

"Vitamin C stops scurvy, what has vitamin C in it?" Finn muttered as searched through the woods. He had brought a bowl with him to collect any berries he might find, but foraging animals had long since eaten any that had remained from the summer. He frantically searched his mind for any source of Vitamin C he could think of. Then he remembered the Pilgrim's dried peas. They had brought them over to plant in the spring. Wouldn't peas have vitamin C? He started to run back to the meeting house to see if he could have some peas when he saw an even better source of Vitamin C—rose hips! There, right in front of him was an old rose bush with rose hips clinging to it. He gathered them all up and ran to the fire where he made a big pot of rose hip tea.

It took many days and many pots of tea before Ginny and the Billington family recovered. Finn also convinced the Pilgrim leaders to let him use some of their peas for soup. Between the rose hips and the peas, the whole family made a complete recovery. Finn knew Ginny would make it when he saw her grinning up at him one day—it was the first time he had seen her smile in weeks.

"Well big brother, looks like you saved my life!"

Finn grinned back at her. "Do you remember what Mom used to say about knowledge?"

"Of course I do," Ginny smiled. "She always used to say that you never know when something you learn will come in useful, so it is important to learn everything you can. Boy was she right; I would never have thought that you reading about scurvy would someday save my life."

"And my life too!" chimed in Aunt Eleanor. Not all of the Pilgrims had been sick with scurvy, so the rose hip tea and peas hadn't saved everyone, but they had saved Ginny and the Billingtons. Things were finally start to look up.

19

A New Friend

Spring was on its way and the days were starting to get a bit longer and warmer. People were still dying, but many more were starting to recover. By the end of March, about half of the Pilgrims had died, including Mary's mother; leaving poor Mary an orphan. Mary herself had been sick, but like Ginny, had recovered. The two girls were sitting outside, enjoying the feel of the sun on their faces and just content to be alive, when they looked up and saw an Indian man dressed in only a breechcloth walk by. They looked at each other in astonishment and then watched as the man walked up to where some of the Pilgrim leaders were standing with muskets in hand and said, "Welcome Englishmen!"

"Ginny, he speaks English!" Mary exclaimed at the same time that Ginny said "Isn't he freezing?" The girls looked at each other and giggled, then turned again to where the Indian man was talking to the Pilgrim leaders. He said his name was Samoset and that he was visiting this area from his home in the north. It was starting to get colder, so Stephen Hopkins ran to get a coat for him while Ginny and Mary found him some cheese, pudding, biscuits, and a piece of duck meat.

As the men spoke, Ginny and Mary hovered nearby so that they could hear what the men were talking about. Samoset told the Pilgrims that about four years earlier every man, woman, and child in the area had died of some sort of plague. Ginny and Mary looked knowingly at each other. They had often discussed why there seemed to be no people living near the settlement, even though there were many empty fields and abandoned houses.

Samoset spent that night at Stephen Hopkins's house and left the next day for the neighboring Indian village, which he said had about sixty people in it. This village was part of the Pokanoket tribe, ruled by the leader or sachem, Massasoit, who lived about sixty miles away. Before the great plague came, Massasoit had ruled around twelve thousand people and had about three thousand warriors. Now, his people were decimated, and he only had a few hundred warriors at his command. This was a huge problem for him because his enemies, the Narragansetts, had not been affected by the plague and had about five thousand fighting men and twenty thousand people. The Narragansetts now considered Massasoit's people and lands as part of their domain, but Massasoit had other plans.

Samoset also solved another mystery for the Pilgrims—why they had been attacked when they first landed. It turned out that a village of Nauset Indians lived near where they had made their first explorations. The Nausets hated the English because of an Englishman named Hunt who had captured a number of their people and sold them as slaves. Because of Hunt, the Nausets were prone to attack any Europeans who landed on their shores.

Later that day, after Samoset had left carrying the gifts that the Pilgrims had given him, the Pilgrims were discussing the Nauset attacks.

"Did you hear what Samoset said about what the Nausets did to the Frenchmen? They slaughtered most of them and took the rest as slaves!" exclaimed Francis Cooke.

"But Francis," said William Brewster, "You haven't told the whole story. The year before that happened, an English ship under the command of a man named Hunt captured a number of Indians to sell as slaves to Spain. The Indians attacked the French in retaliation. They didn't know the difference between a Frenchman and an Englishman."

"That still doesn't make it right to attack one group of people because another group did something bad," Francis exclaimed. "That would be like me attacking you because your friend Bradford did something to me."

"No, that wouldn't be right," agreed William, "but knowing what had been done to them does make it a bit more understandable. That evil man Hunt has caused a lot of misery and bad feelings in this part of the world. We need to show the natives that not all Englishmen are like that. We will need to be extra careful in our dealings with them and make sure that we are fair in all things."

20

Massasoit

The following day Samoset returned with
five other men. Finn saw them as they walked
bravely into the village. They were wearing some
type of cloth leggings with leather breechcloths
tied around their waists. One of them had a wild-
cat skin over his arm. The Pilgrims hurried to
make the newcomers welcome and offered them
food and drink. Finn watched as these two cul-
tures came together in friendship and was
amazed. The Indians sang and danced for the
Pilgrims, who weren't quite sure what to make of
this foreign-style of dancing. The Indians also returned the tools that had been stolen earlier and
arrangements were made for them to come back
another day to trade animal skins. The five men

left, but Samoset stayed behind and lived with the Pilgrims for three more days. When the other Indians didn't return, the Pilgrim leaders asked Samoset to go to them and see what was taking them so long. Before he left, they gave him a hat, stockings, shoes, a shirt, and some cloth. Finn realized that these items were precious not only to the Indians, to whom they were novelties, but also to the Pilgrims, who no longer had easy access to the basic necessities.

Samoset returned the following afternoon, bringing with him Squanto who, though not a Nauset, was one of the Indians that Hunt had kidnapped. Finn was in awe. He remembered reading about Squanto when he was younger, and now here he was right in front of him! Squanto had lived in England for a time and could speak English. He had made his way back to America, only to find that his whole village had been wiped out by the plague. His native village used to be right near where the Pilgrims were living now.

Samoset and Squanto had brought with them a few skins to trade, but the big excitement was that they brought word that the great sachem Massasoit and about sixty followers were on their way and would be arriving shortly at Plymouth.

Soon, Massasoit and his men appeared on top of the next hill. And there they stayed. Both the Indians and the Pilgrims were nervous of each other, and neither side was willing to risk sending their leaders to the other.

As Finn and Francis stood nearby and watched the two groups eye each other across the valley, Finn turned to Francis and muttered "I'm afraid that they will lose their chance to make peace with each other because both sides are too afraid to make the first move."

Then Squanto brought a message from Massasoit asking for someone to parley with him. After conferring awhile, the Pilgrims decided to send Edward Winslow. The next thing Finn knew, Master Winslow was beckoning to him to come along! He soon found himself hurrying after Master Winslow, carrying the gifts for the sacham.

Master Winslow and Finn went up to Massasoit and presented the gifts. Then Finn stood respectfully off to the side while Master Winslow gave a speech telling Massasoit that King James saluted him, and would like to make peace with him, and have him as a friend and ally. Massasoit seemed pleased with both the gifts and the speech and indicated that Master Winslow was to stay here as a hostage, while Massasoit went with twenty warriors to meet with the other Pilgrim leaders; leaving their bows and arrows behind. The adults seemed to have forgotten about Finn, so he followed the Indians back to the village.

When they reached Plymouth, Francis sidled up to Finn and whispered, "They have been discussing over and over how to greet Massasoit when he gets here. They want to make a strong impression on him, so that he will feel like we will be good allies for him."

Finn watched as Massasoit was led into one of the houses where a green rug had been laid on the floor with some cushions around it. Next the Pilgrim's governor, John Carver, appeared with a drum and trumpet playing and some soldiers marching along. The two leaders greeted each other and sat down to negotiate a peace treaty that would last over fifty years.

The Peace Treaty
(From Mourt's Relation)

1. *That neyther he nor any of his should injure or doe hurt to any of our people.*

2. *And if any of his did hurt to any of ours, he should send the offender, that we might punish him.*

3. *That if any of our Tooles were taken away when our people were at worke, he should cause them to be restored, and if ours did any harme to any of his, wee whould doe the like to them.*

4. *If any did unjustly warre against him, we would ayde him; If any did warre against us, he should ayde us.*

5. *He should send to his neighbour Confederates, to certifie them of this, that they might not wrong us, but might be likewise comprsed in the conditions of Peace.*

6. *That when their men came to us, they should leave their Bowes and Arrowes behind them, as wee should doe our Peeces when we came to them.*

Lastly, that doing thus, King James would esteeme of him as his friend and Alie

21

Squanto

The days following the signing of the peace treaty were unlike any that Finn had experienced in the New World so far. The Mayflower had left for England, leaving the small group of Pilgrims on their own. Then, shortly after the Mayflower left, their beloved Governor Carver suddenly died. And, now that the Pilgrims had made peace with their Indian neighbors, it was not an unusual sight to see Indian braves in the woods or to see Ginny serving food to one or more members of Massasoit's tribe.

One day as she was walking away from one of those meals, Finn suddenly realized something. "Ginny, have you noticed that we seem to have more food lately?" he asked.

Ginny looked over at Finn somberly. "Finn, we have more food because half of us died. We don't need to ration as much now. But if we don't have a good harvest, it will be back to rationing again in the fall. Plus, all of these unexpected Indian guests are starting to take a heavy toll on our food supply."

Increasing the food supply was on everyone's mind. Spring was finally here, the days were getting warmer, and every able-bodied person was helping with the spring planting. They were helped greatly in this by Squanto, who continued to live with the Pilgrims and was teaching them how to grow corn by planting the seeds in mounds of dirt with a fish buried in them to help fertilize the young shoots. Squanto also showed them many other things, and one day he took Finn down to the river to fish for eels. Finn watched as Squanto scared them out of their holes with his feet and then grabbed them as they swam away.

As they were walking home with their catch, Finn said, "I'm glad that Massasoit made a peace treaty with us. It would have been awful if we had all been fighting."

"The peace treaty is good for Massasoit too," replied Squanto. "This way he has an ally against the Narragansetts who will be afraid of your muskets." After walking a little further Squanto added, "And I am also glad that we are not fighting. The people of my village are lost, but you are here now and have given me a home. I am happy to teach you our ways."

That night, they all had a fine meal of the eels that Squanto and Finn had caught.

22

A Visit to Massasoit

They are eating us from house and home!" exclaimed Stephen Hopkins. "Every time I turn around there is another family of Indians visiting us that expect to be fed. We need to do something about it before we don't have any food left!"

"Yes, but what do you suggest we do about it?" asked the Pilgrim's new governor, William Bradford.

"I think that we should send a delegation to Massasoit's village, and explain to him that we are still a young village, and that we do not yet know how our corn crop will fair, so we do not have enough food to feed all of the visitors we are getting from his tribe."

The governor looked at Stephen uneasily. "Are you sure of this? We don't want to inadvertently insult him. That could have horrible repercussions. He may decide to attack us or something."

Edward Winslow spoke up, "I think Master Hopkins is right. If we ask politely and with great respect, surely Massasoit will understand. But we should also let him know that he is always welcome in our village; it is just that we cannot support so many visitors at this time. I suggest that we give him a copper chain and any of his special friends that he gives the chain to will be invited into our village and fed, but no one else will be. Hopefully this will slow down the amount of people that we have to feed."

The governor looked thoughtfully at the two men. "Perhaps you are correct. It would also be a good opportunity to ask him how we can find the owners of that corn that we borrowed in our need so that we can repay them. I think that since you two have come up with this good suggestion, that you should be the ones to form this delegation. Squanto should also go to guide you and translate." At that moment the Governor's eyes rested on Finn, who had been sitting in the corner listening to the conversation. "And why don't you take young Finn here with you? He has shown himself to be a helpful lad on previous expeditions."

Finn looked up in excitement, "I'd love to go!" he exclaimed.

However, when Ginny heard about the expedition, she was not so excited. "I hate it when you go on these expeditions," she said worriedly. "Last time you almost got killed."

"But we're friends with the Indians now; I won't be in any danger." Finn replied. "Please don't be upset Ginny; it's a chance of a lifetime. I'll get to see a real seventeenth century Indian village."

"I know," Ginny sighed. "I just wish I could go with you."

Finn looked at her thoughtfully, "You know, it really is unfair that you don't get to go on these adventures. Maybe we can sneak you along somehow. Do you think you can follow us and stay out of sight until it's too late to send you back alone?"

"I'm not sure," said Ginny. "If it was just Masters Winslow and Hopkins, I think I could, but Squanto will be with you, and you know how good he is in the woods. I bet he would notice and send me back."

"You're probably right," Finn sighed. "He most likely would notice you. We'll have to wait and try it sometime when he's not going along."

"Well, at least I'll have more time to spend with Mary," said Ginny. "I am really going to miss her when we go back to our time."

* * * *

A couple of days later, Finn found himself walking through the woods behind Stephen Hopkins. It was surprisingly easy going, and Squanto explained that the Indians regularly burned the underbrush in this area of the forest to make it easier to travel through. It was early July and a fine warm day to be walking through the woods. The plan was to spend the first night in Namschet; an Indian village that they knew must be fairly close, since its inhabitants often visited Plymouth. As they were walking along, Finn heard talking up ahead and looked up to see about ten Indian men, women, and children; most of them familiar faces from their frequent visits to Plymouth. After many friendly greetings, the group decided to accompany them to Namaschet, which they reached at around three-o'clock that afternoon. As they walked into the village, the first thing Finn noticed was the round huts, or wetu, scattered around. They looked like large balls cut in half with mats placed over them.

The villagers were very happy to see them since it was the first time any of the Pilgrims had visited their village. They shared a meal together of corn bread, acorn mush and fish eggs. As he ate, Finn thought about how much he had changed in the last few months. Before coming on this adventure, he would have turned his nose up at most of the food he now ate without question. "Hunger certainly makes everything taste better," he thought to himself.

After the meal the villagers asked if the Pilgrims could use one of their muskets to kill a crow that had been eating their corn. The Pilgrims obliged, and the villagers were much impressed with the shot. At this point Squanto suggested that the Pilgrims continue on to the next village instead of stopping for the night, so it was decided to keep going a few more miles. They reached the next village as the sun was setting and shared a meal of fish with the villagers. Finn was surprised to see that this village had no huts to sleep in; everyone slept out in an open field, even though the villagers lived there all summer.

* * * *

Finn woke up the next morning and heard Edward Winslow and Squanto talking in low voices. Squanto had a sad look on his face as he said, "Once thousands of men lived here, but the great plague took them all."

"I had noticed all of the empty fields," replied Master Winslow. "It is sad to see all of these fields with no one left to tend them. I am very sorry for your people's loss."

Squanto nodded in acknowledgement and then indicated that they should probably get started. The small group moved on, this time accompanied by six Indian guides from the village. After walking about five miles, they came to a river and started to cross it.

Suddenly, out of nowhere, there came a great yelling and two men charged at them with bows drawn. Finn nearly fell into the water in surprise, but it turned out that they were friends of the Indians who accompanied them.

"Did you notice how brave they were?" exclaimed Stephen. "They were heavily outnumbered, but they still were ready to attack us if we were enemies. These are an admirable people."

Eventually, the group reached Massasoit's village, but he was not at home and had to be sent for. When he arrived, the Pilgrims saluted him with their muskets, passed on their message, and gave him the copper chain and a red coat. Then it was Massasoit's turn to make a speech, which to Finn seemed to go on forever. He kept waiting for someone to offer them some food, since the Pilgrims had given away or eaten all of theirs as they passed through the various villages on the way, but it turned out that since Massasoit and his people had just arrived here themselves, they didn't have any food either. This village did have some huts however, and the Pilgrims slept that night in the same hut with Massasoit. Their beds were planks that were about a foot off the ground with mats and skins laid over them. Finn was used to sleeping without a mattress by now, so the bed was comfortable enough, but it turned out that the Indians would sing themselves to sleep, something he was not used to. To make matters worse, the beds were full of lice and fleas, not an uncommon occurrence for the seventeenth century, but something that he was definitely not used to. He had a very hard time falling asleep that night.

The next day more visitors arrived, and the day was spent playing gambling games for skins and knives. One of these games, called Hubbub, was played by tossing pieces of bones in a bowl and winning points by how they fell. After that, the villagers asked the Pilgrims to shoot at a target with their muskets.

It was now around one o'clock and so when Finn saw Massasoit approach with some fish, he was happy to finally see some food. Then he realized that there were only two fish that were going to be split between about forty people.

That night Finn not only went to bed hungry, but it was another miserable night in the hut. The Pilgrims had thought about sleeping outside, but the mosquitoes were particularly bad here, so sleeping outside of the hut wasn't much of an option.

Finn wasn't the only one who had a hard time sleeping. Just before dawn, Masters Winslow and Hopkins took him aside and said, "We'll be leaving for Plymouth today Finn. We haven't had anything to eat but that small amount of fish for almost two days now, and we're afraid that between lack of food and lack of sleep, that we won't make it home without collapsing."

They left immediately and made it to the next village where they were given a small amount of fish and were able to trade for a little parched corn. Later, their Indian guides were able to catch some fish, so things got less desperate-feeling, though on their last night out it started to rain, and continued raining until they finally reached Plymouth the next day, wet, weary, and very glad to be home.

23

Rescuing John

Finn did you hear what happened?" Ginny exclaimed as Finn came walking up after a long day gathering reeds for thatching a roof. "Cousin John is lost! No one has seen him since early this morning. All of the men are out searching for him!"

Finn immediately thought of the horrible time when he'd been lost in the woods with John Goodman and Peter. At least he'd had company while he was lost, poor Cousin John was all alone.

"Let's go help look for him," he exclaimed. But even though Finn, Ginny and many others searched for the next few days, Cousin John was nowhere to be found. Aunt Eleanor walked around in a daze, crying at odd moments, and Uncle John woke up early every morning and spent all day in the woods calling Cousin John's name. A week went by, and their hope was dwindling.

Then, just when they thought all was lost, word came to the village that Cousin John was alive and well and being cared for in a Nauset village. He had wandered around in the woods lost for about five days until he came upon an Indian village. The sachem of that village sent him to the Nausets—the same people who had attacked the Pilgrims when they first landed.

"The Nausets!" Aunt Eleanor exclaimed as she burst into tears. "They'll kill him for sure, my poor boy!"

Governor Bradford immediately put together an expedition in the shallop to retrieve John.

"Perhaps we can take this opportunity to try and arrange a peace agreement with the Nausets," he said. "And maybe we can finally find the owner of the corn we took when we first landed."

This expedition was much larger than the one to Massasoit's village, since they didn't know what to expect. Finn and Uncle John were part of the expedition.

The first day out the shallop was caught in a thunderstorm, so they pulled into a harbor for the night and slept in the boat.

* * * *

The next morning they saw some Indians catching lobsters who invited the Pilgrims to come and eat with them before they went on their way. The Pilgrims agreed, and the Indians brought them to meet their young sachem, Iyanough, who impressed the Pilgrims with his gentle and courteous manner. Suddenly, Finn noticed an old woman who kept looking at them and crying. He nudged Uncle John and pointed her out.

"What is she crying about?" asked Uncle John.

"Her three sons were captured by the Englishman Hunt and taken to Spain. She has never seen them again," replied Squanto. "You people remind her of her loss." The Pilgrims sat shocked and silent.

After a moment Edward Winslow said, "Would you please tell her from us how sorry we are for what he did. He was a bad man, and all the Englishmen who heard of his offence condemned him for it."

"Hunt has much to account for," commented Uncle John. "His deplorable actions have ruined relations between our people and theirs. I hate to think that these people believe that all Englishmen are like the despicable Hunt."

"All we can do is make sure that our own actions reflect better on our countrymen," replied Winslow. "Let us at least give this poor woman some gifts, though they will not make up for the loss of her sons."

Shortly after, Iyanough and two of his men decided to accompany the Pilgrims on the rest of their journey. When they reached the land of the Nauset, the day was almost over and the tide was low, so they could not bring the shallop close to shore. This suited the Pilgrims well, since after their last experience here, they did not totally trust the Nausets not to attack them. Iyanough and his men waded ashore along with Squanto to let the Nausets know that the Pilgrims had arrived.

While they waited, Uncle John sat strained and tense next to Finn in the shallop. "I just hope John is safe and that we can bring him back home to his mother," he said.

"I'm sure he is," reassured Finn. "You will be seeing him soon; I just know it."

Then Squanto waded out to the shallop with a group of Indians who slowly surrounded the boat. Squanto came up to Captain Standish and murmured, "The man whose corn you took last year is here. I know you've been trying to find out who it belonged to, so I brought him back with me."

The Captain let that man and one other on board, and Edward Winslow spoke to the man about getting payment to him for the corn.

Suddenly, Finn heard Uncle John gasp. He looked up and saw about fifty Indians wading out to the boat, Cousin John among them. Another

fifty remained on shore with their bows and arrows ready. It appeared that the Pilgrims weren't
the only ones who were unsure of their welcome!
Aspinet, the sachem of the Nausets, greeted
them and then entered the boat along with John.
While Finn and Uncle John fussed over John,
Aspinet sat with the Pilgrim leaders discussing a
peace agreement.

After the Nausets had left, Captain Standish
ordered the men to get underway immediately.
The Nauset sachem had told them that Massasoit had been captured by the Narragansetts,
and since most of the strongest men of the colony
were on board the shallop, they were worried
about what was happening back at Plymouth if
their friend and ally was in trouble.

24

Rescuing Squanto

While they were trying to find more information on what was happening with Massasoit, Hobbamock, an Indian friend of the Pilgrims came running into the village, gasping for breath.

"Squanto has been captured and probably killed!" he gasped. He went on to explain that both he and Squanto had been captured by a minor sachem under Massasoit named Coubatant, who did not approve of Massasoit's friendship with the Pilgrims. Coubatant wanted to kill Squanto because if Squanto was dead, "the English would lose their tongue." Hobbamock had managed to escape and had run to the Pilgrims for help.

Instantly pandemonium broke out. Squanto had been a good friend to the Pilgrims, and it was immediately decided to avenge his death, not only because of the Pilgrim's friendship with Squanto, but because if their enemies saw that they did not protect and avenge their friends, then they would soon lose the respect and friendship of the various tribes they had made peace with.

Finn watched sadly as Captain Standish and fourteen men went on their mission. After losing so many friends this winter, it was especially hard to lose Squanto, just when it seemed like all of the dying was over. Suddenly he was filled with anger over the senselessness of this death. To kill Squanto just because he was their friend! But what if Squanto was still alive? Hobbamock didn't know for sure that Squanto had been killed. How Finn wished he could go with the men and see for himself! Maybe if Squanto was alive, he could help him somehow.

Then Finn remembered his conversation with Ginny a few weeks back about trying to sneak along on an expedition. Without thinking further about it, he immediately started following after the men. He had observed how Squanto walked quietly in the woods all summer and tried to copy how he had seen Squanto move as he walked.

It was a wet, cold night, and after a while Finn began to have second thoughts about what he had done. However, it was too late to go back since he had no idea where he was. He plodded along cursing himself for his stupidity. What was he thinking following the men like this? Captain Standish would be furious when he found out. And what did he think he could do to help anyhow?

Just then Finn realized that he couldn't hear the men up ahead. "Great," he said to himself. "Now I'll get lost in the woods and cause even more trouble." At that moment he realized that he couldn't hear the men because they had all stopped up ahead and were silently staring at him.

Captain Standish stepped forward. "Young man, just what do you think you are doing? This is a military operation and is no place for boys."

Finn hung his head. "I'm sorry sir. I just wasn't thinking. I was so worried about Squanto and I wanted to do something to help."

Uncle John spoke up. "Finn, did you tell anyone where you were going?"

Finn looked at his feet, "no sir."

Uncle John looked furious. "Do you realize how worried your Aunt is going to be? She just got over worrying about John and now she'll be frantic about you. And what about your poor sister? She's going to be worried too. I don't know what got into you boy; you're usually not so thoughtless."

Captain Standish spoke up. "What's done is done, and there's not much we can do about it now. Finn, I want you to stay at the end of the group, next to your uncle. Do exactly as you are told and don't make a sound."

"Yes sir," Finn replied faintly. He got into line behind Uncle John and quietly moved on with the rest of the group.

After a long weary hike, the group of men stopped just outside of the town of Nemaschet and had a quick bit to eat.

"Finn, I want you to stay here with our knapsacks. We will meet you here when our operation is complete," ordered Captain Standish.

Finn nodded and watched as the men slipped away into the darkness. Not too long after he heard people yelling and crying; and then two shots rang out. He huddled down next to the knapsacks as the rain dripped down his neck and wished with all his heart that he hadn't followed the men. While he was sitting there feeling sorry for himself, Uncle John came up quietly next to him.

"It's over Finn, you can come into the village now," said Uncle John.

"I'm sorry Uncle John; I didn't mean to make so much trouble."

"Well, let's just be glad that it all turned out well," replied Uncle John. "Sometimes the only thing you can do when you've done something wrong is learn from your mistake and never do it again."

"Don't worry about that," said Finn. "I certainly won't do this again. What happened in the village? I heard musket shots. Did you find Squanto?"

Uncle John grinned. "We sure did! He's alive and well! It turns out that Coubatant didn't kill him after all; he changed his mind for some reason. Coubatant has disappeared, but a couple of villagers were injured in the ruckus. Nothing serious though. We'll bring them to Master Fuller in the morning, and he'll set them right. In the meantime we're going to stay here for the night. Help me gather up these packs and let's head on over there."

The next morning, Captain Standish gave a speech to the villagers saying that if Coubatant kept threatening the Pilgrims, who had kindly entertained him and had never intended evil toward him, that there was no place he could go that would be safe from them. And if Massasoit was not returned safely from the Narragansetts or if any of the Pilgrim's Indian friends were harmed, that they would avenge them.

Finn and the men returned to the village that evening and Finn had to face an angry sister and aunt. Over the next few weeks, various sachems indicated that they would like to make peace with the Pilgrims. Massasoit returned, and it appeared that Captain Standish's raid on Coubatant's village was a success in that it strengthened the relationship with the Pilgrim's friends and earned the respect and friendship of their enemies. On September thirteenth, nine sachems, including Coubatant, came to Plymouth to sign a peace treaty. The Pilgrims had achieved their goal of establishing peaceful relations with their Indian neighbors.

25

The Harvest Festival

Ginny stretched her back and groaned. "I never knew farming was such hard work," she said.

"Yes, but we are almost all done," replied Finn. "Twenty acres of corn and six of barley and peas; all harvested and ready for winter."

"Well, maybe not the peas," laughed Ginny. "They pretty much all died on the vine. I felt bad about taking the Indian's corn when we first came here, but if we hadn't, we never would have been able to grow enough peas and barley to survive."

"I'm glad that they were finally able to find the owner of the corn and pay him for it," replied Finn.

"Yes, things are much better now. We have more food, the people are healthier, and we have made friends with the various Indian tribes. It's amazing to think of what we've accomplished in less than a year," said Ginny.

Later that evening the Pilgrim leaders announced that they were going to send four men out to the marshes to shoot enough ducks and geese for a feast so that everyone could celebrate the successful harvest. These four men shot enough birds in one day to feed the whole village for a week; a week that was filled with food, games, music, and fun. Massasoit was invited, and he came with ninety of his followers, bringing five deer to the feast.

At one point, Ginny walked over to Finn, where he was waiting his turn at a game of Quoits and said, "Finn, you do know what this is, don't you?"

"What do you mean?"

"This is the first Thanksgiving!" Ginny exclaimed. "We're here at the first Thanksgiving!"

Finn laughed. "You're right, I hadn't even thought of that. It's so different from how I pictured it, much more fun and natural," he said. "After all of our hard work and suffering this year, it just feels like it's time to celebrate that we survived!"

"Do you know what this also means?" said Ginny somberly. It means that we've been here a full year. We'll be going home soon."

Finn sighed, "It has been both a horrible and a wonderful year. It's a shame to have to leave now that things are getting better here, but it will be great to get back home."

"I know," replied Ginny quietly. "I know."

26

The Fortune

To Arms, to Arms!" The call rang out across the village. The cannon was fired and the men ran in from their work to see what was the matter. A ship had been spotted and it was not known if it was friend or foe. It could be the French coming to wipe out the small settlement before it got too large. Every man and boy was handed a musket, including Finn. He was glad that he had learned to shoot this year, though he hoped that it wouldn't come to that. He didn't remember any French attacks from his history books, so he was hoping that this was a false alarm.

To his relief it turned out to be an English ship, the Fortune, coming with more settlers for

Plymouth.

Ginny came running over to where Finn was putting his musket away. "Finally, a ship from England! Everyone has been waiting and hoping that the company would send more supplies for the winter, and it looks like they finally have," she said excitedly. "I wonder what they brought."

But Ginny's hopes were soon dashed, along with everyone else's. The ship brought absolutely no supplies, just thirty-seven passengers, enough to almost double the size of the colony. With only seven houses built and four public buildings, it was going to be hard to find a place for everyone to sleep. To make matters worse, just when the Pilgrims had been feeling like they had enough food to comfortably get through the winter, they were going to have to cut their rations in half, and even then they would only have enough corn to last six months.

But there were also cries of joy, as family and friends who had been separated for over a year greeted each other.

Just then, Finn glanced over at William Bradford who was reading a letter and getting more and more agitated as he read it. Edward Winslow also noticed Bradford and asked what was wrong.

"This letter was sent to poor Governor Carver, who is no longer with us. They are accusing us of shirking in our duties because we didn't fill the Mayflower with goods before it left for England!"

he exclaimed. "We lost half of our friends last winter and most of us were deathly ill, and they accuse us of not working hard enough," he said indignantly. "I am going to write to them immediately and set the record straight!" Finn stared at him in astonishment as he remembered the hardships and accomplishments of the past year. How could anyone accuse the Pilgrims of shirking their duties? They had endured against all odds and not only survived, but had established friendly relations with their neighbors, grown a successful crop, and started building a village. The people in England had no idea what it was like here.

27

The Adventure Ends

A few days after the arrival of the Fortune, Ginny pulled Finn aside and whispered, "The time-remote says that we have one more day left here. We'll need to make sure that we are together tomorrow. I'd hate for one of us to go back and the other to be left here in the past."

"You're right," said Finn thoughtfully. "I think the best thing would be for us to wake up early and go hide in the woods until the remote sends us home."

"I think we'd better not even go to sleep," said Ginny. "What if the remote sends us home right after midnight?"

The twins made their plans and spent the rest of the day visiting their special friends. Ginny spent most of the day with Mary, though it was difficult not being able to tell Mary that she would never see her again.

"I wonder if she will notice that I am gone and worry about me," thought Ginny, "Or will it be like I was never here? I guess it really doesn't matter; either way, I'm losing a friend tomorrow."

The two saddened and subdued twins quietly closed the door to the Billington cabin late that night and crept into the woods. Finn had brought a stout stick in case they encountered wolves, but Ginny didn't feel very protected, and she wished he'd been able to bring one of the muskets.

"We'd better hold hands so that we don't get separated in the transfer," she said as she slipped her hand into Finn's. "I'm going to miss all of our friends here, aren't you?"

"Yes," said Finn shortly. "But at least they won't have to feed us this winter. With the new folks from the Fortune here, they certainly don't need two extra mouths to feed!"

"Is food all you ever think about? teased Ginny.

"Of course not," grinned Finn in the dark, "but won't you be glad to have some of Aunt Martha's fried chicken?"

"Or how about her blueberry pie?" countered Ginny.

And that was when it happened...the world started swirling. Ginny gripped Finn's hand tighter as the nausea crashed over her. She closed her eyes and the next thing she knew she was laying on the living room floor and Finn was shaking her.

"Ginny, open your eyes, are you alright?"

She opened first one eye, then the next. "Are we home? Did we make it?"

"We sure did!" Finn laughed. "Come on, let's raid the kitchen!"

A couple of hours later, Aunt Martha and Uncle Peter came home. They were carrying bags of groceries and a big turkey. "Kids, come help unload the car, I've bought everything for our Thanksgiving feast!"

Ginny and Finn just looked at each other and grinned.

Historical Notes

Finn, Ginny, and the other modern-day characters in this book are fictitious, but all of the characters from the seventeenth century in this story were real people. The historical events in this story are based on the Pilgrims own accounts as related in two books: *Mourt's Relation*, and *History of Plymouth Plantation*.

While we do have excellent descriptions of the Pilgrim's adventures, and in some cases their thoughts on certain matters (for example their concern about paying the Indians back for the corn that the Pilgrims had stolen or their discomfort while sleeping in Massasoit's wetu), we don't know their exact conversations. This means that all of the conversations in this book are fictitious, though the content of some of them is taken from incidents in one of the two books mentioned above. So while most of the incidents in this book did actually happen, the conversations associated with them are fiction. And of course, the Pilgrims didn't use the same speech patterns that we use today, but I chose to write the book using modern speech patterns to make it easier to read for the modern young reader. Readers who are interested in researching the actual incidents in the Pilgrim's own words can find *Mourt's Relation* and the *History of Plymouth Plantation* available for free online at: http://books.google.com/

There were a couple of other expeditions that were not covered in the book. One of them is mentioned briefly; the expedition where the Pilgrims went back for more of the Indian's corn. This expedition is something of a puzzle because in the Pilgrim's first expedition they were careful not to disturb the Indian grave that they found, but in the next expedition, they actually dug up a grave and discovered the bones of what appeared to be a European man. On this expedition they also took items from some Indian huts. They intended to leave some gifts in exchange behind, but forgot to in their haste to get back. Whether they repaid the owners later when they paid for the corn is unknown. All in all, the Pilgrims appear to have tried to be fair in their dealings with the Indians they encountered, but on this particular expedition they seem to have been more thoughtless in their behavior than they were the rest of the time.

The hardships endured by the Pilgrims were real. About half of them died in their first few months in America from various illnesses, scurvy being one of them. However Ginny and the Billington's miraculous recovery by drinking rose hip tea and eating peas is pure fiction. It is possible that some of the scurvy victims started to recover as more fresh food was available in the spring, but there is no way of knowing that now. What is known is that the Billington family was one of the few Mayflower families to survive that first year without losing any family members.

The Billington family members are actually ancestors not only of Finn and Ginny, but also of mine. They are an interesting family; they were among the "Strangers" who were on the Mayflower along with the group of religious separatists who first conceived of the voyage. Unfortunately the Billington family did not always see eye to eye with the Pilgrim leaders. All of the Billington males managed to get into trouble that first year in America: Francis almost set the Mayflower on fire, young John got lost in the woods and had to be rescued, and their father got on the wrong side of Miles Standish and almost had his neck and heels tied together for it. The reason for this quarrel with Miles Standish has been lost in time and the conversation that Ginny witnesses between John Billington and Miles Standish is pure speculation on my part. The *History of Plymouth Plantation* only says that *"The first offence committed in the colony was by Billington, in 1621, who, for contempt of the Captain's lawful command, with opprobrious speeches, was adjusted to have his neck and heels tied together."* This punishment was never carried out.

Francis Billington is the only child of John and Eleanor who survived to have children of his own. His brother, John Billington Jr., died sometime between 1627 and 1630, and John Billington Sr. was executed for murder in 1630.

Ginny's friend Mary Chilton married John Winslow, younger brother of Pilgrim Edward Winslow and lived until 1679 after having ten children.

William Bradford married again in 1623, which was also the year that the Pilgrims decided that communal ownership of their land wasn't working, so they assigned private property to each settler. Bradford reported that this had the immediate and desired effect of increasing the crops planted as the settlers worked harder when they were allowed to work for themselves, instead of just for the community. Bradford was Plymouth's governor for all but about five years until he died in 1657.

Steven Hopkins had a most adventurous life. He was shipwrecked in Bermuda, arrested for mutiny and sentenced to death, escaped his death sentence, went on to Jamestown and lived there for a number of years during one of its worst periods. Then his wife, who was living in England, died so he returned to England to take care of his children. There he re-married and in 1620 decided to accompany the Pilgrims on their voyage to the New World, where he died in 1644.

Squanto's relationship with the Pilgrims was more complex than many people know. His invaluable assistance during that first year was a big factor in the Pilgrim's survival, but in fact, Squanto needed the Pilgrims as much as they needed him. He was not completely trusted by

Massasoit,[3] with good reason as it turned out, and the Pilgrims provided him with a home and friendship. However, it gradually dawned on the Pilgrims that Squanto was a bit of a troublemaker. One of the first signs of this occurred during that first year when a group of Pilgrims made an expedition to visit the Massachusetts tribe.

Squanto came along as their guide and when they finally did meet some members of the tribe, he urged the Pilgrims to steal their furs and other items because *"they are a bad people, and haue oft threatned you."* The Pilgrims declined to take Squanto's advice, but this was a perhaps one of the first signs that Squanto was not to be totally trusted.

It turned out that Squanto was ambitious and wanted to take over Massasoit's position. Sometime during the Pilgrim's second winter in America (and possibly before), he started scaring the local Indians with stories of how the Pilgrims could summon the plague at will and convinced them that he could keep this from happening. More and more of the local villages began looking to Squanto for leadership in dealing with the Pilgrims. Then Squanto put the second part of his plan in action. He sent a relative of his running

---

[3] Massasoit is actually a title which means "Great Sachem," not a name, but I use the name Massasoit throughout the book because that is what the Pilgrims called him, and that is the name that many history books call him. His real name was Ousamequin.

into Plymouth saying that Massasoit had joined with the Narragansetts and was coming to attack the village.

Luckily for both the Pilgrims and Massasoit, another Indian, Hobbamock, who had been living with them at Plymouth for the winter, had warned them of Squanto's treachery. The Pilgrims didn't want to believe it at first, but when Squanto's relative came running into town with his story of a pending attack by Massasoit, the Pilgrims realized that it could be a ploy to try and get *them* to attack Massasoit. Hobbamock's wife offered to go to Massasoit's village to see if he was planning an attack and found out that he wasn't. Massasoit was furious with Squanto's treachery and insisted that the Pilgrims send Squanto to him to be executed. Governor Bradford, remembering all of the help that Squanto had given them during that first difficult year, refused. This refusal caused a rift between the Pilgrims and Massasoit that would be hard to repair. Squanto himself died less than a year later.

The rift with Massasoit was finally healed in 1623 when Edward Winslow helped cure Massasoit when he was deathly ill. At that time, Massasoit told Winslow that the Massachusetts Indians were fed up with the inhabitants of Wessagusset, a recent English settlement. They were so fed up that they were planning to attack both Wessagusset and Plymouth and kill all of the inhabitants. Massasoit told the Pilgrims that they needed to kill the ringleaders of this plot immediately, before the warriors were assembled to attack. After much deliberation, the Pilgrims decided to put their trust in Massasoit and sent Captain Standish and a small number of men on an expedition to kill the ringleaders. The ultimate results of this action greatly increased Massasoit's power in the region. Massasoit had finally achieved his goal; by joining with the Pilgrims, he had strengthened his power and protected his people.

Squanto and Massasoit's relationship with the Pilgrims was not as simple as many Pilgrim accounts would have it, and the rich tale of the Pilgrim's adventures has often been simplified or distorted in modern times to the point where many people don't even know the true story. I hope that this book will help to bring their story to a new generation.

Susan Kilbride, 2012

Bibliography

Books Written by the Pilgrims:
Mourt's Relation
or Journal of the Plantation at Plymouth
Written by various Pilgrims in 1622 and
available for free online at: http://books.google.com/

History of Plymouth Plantation
Written between 1630 & 1640 by William Bradford
and available for free online at: http://books.google.com/

Books Written about the Pilgrims:

The Times of Their Lives
by James Deetz and Patricia Scott Deetz
Anchor Books, 2000

Here Shall I Die Ashore
by Caleb H. Johnson, Xlibris Corporation, 2007

The Mayflower and Her Passengers
by Caleb H. Johnson, Xlibris Corporation, 2006

Mayflower
by Nathaniel Philbrick, Penguin Books, 2006

Websites:
The Plymouth Colony Archive Project
by Patricia Scott Deetz & Christopher Fennell
http://www.histarch.uiuc.edu/plymouth/framing02.html

Building a Home
Plimoth Plantation Website
http://www.plimoth.org/learn/just-kids/homework-
help/building-home

17707099R00080

Made in the USA
Lexington, KY
07 October 2012